Kabir

Selected Couplets from the Sakhi in Transversion

Kabir

*Selected Couplets from the Sakhi
in Transversion*
(400-Odd verses in Iambic Tetrameter Stanza Form)

MOHAN SINGH KARKI

MOTILAL BANARSIDASS PUBLISHERS
PRIVATE LIMITED ● DELHI

First Edition: Delhi, 2001

ISBN: 81-208-1788-5 (Cloth)
ISBN: 81-208-1799-0 (Paper)

Also available at:

MOTILAL BANARSIDASS

236, 9th Main III Block, Jayanagar, Bangalore 560 011
41 U.A. Bungalow Road, Jawahar Nagar, Delhi 110 007
8 Mahalaxmi Chamber, Warden Road, Mumbai 400 026
120 Royapettah High Road, Mylapore, Chennai 600 004
Sanas Plaza, 1302 Baji Rao Road, Pune 411 002
8 Camac Street, Kolkata 700 017
Ashok Rajpath, Patna 800 004
Chowk, Varanasi 221 001

Printed in India
BY JAINENDRA PRAKASH JAIN AT SHRI JAINENDRA PRESS,
A-45 NARAINA, PHASE-I, NEW DELHI 110 028
AND PUBLISHED BY NARENDRA PRAKASH JAIN FOR
MOTILAL BANARSIDASS PUBLISHERS PRIVATE LIMITED,
BUNGALOW ROAD, DELHI 110 007

Preface

Kabir's Greatness as poet-saint or saint-poet is unparalleled in the whole range of Hindi literature. In the history of Hindi literature of some 1200 years no other poet, excepting Tulsidas, equals the genius of Kabir nor does equal the greatness of Kabir. For Hindus he is a *vaishnav* and for Muslims he is a Pir (Muslim saint). The followers of Kabir regard him as an incarnation of divinity. Modern nationalists regard him the pioneer of Hindu-Muslim unity. For neo-*vedantists* he is a philanthropist. For progressive thinkers Kabir is a social-reformer. He is a heretic, and, at the same time, a liberal thinker. In terms of religious philosophy he is a monotheist—the devotee of the Unconditioned or the Absolute. In leading a domestic life he was a yogi, and, in his vocation of weaving he was a philosopher who, like Wordsworth's skylark, was 'true to the kindred points of heaven and home'. Western thinkers call him an Indian Martin Luther. In his multisided genius Kabir is unparalleled.

In taking up the work of transversion of Kabir's *Dohas* (Hindi couplets) from the *Sakhi* I was primarily inspired by Fitzgerald's work *Rubaiyat of Omar Khayyam*. I felt oriental wisdom should be made available to English-speaking readers who want to enjoy verse with the message of Kabir. When the work was midway I came across the *Gita*'s blank verse translation by Sir Edwin Arnold, and, much later, I came across the free verse translation of Kabir's one hundred poems (songs) by Rabindranath Tagore.

Some three years ago when I made my initial attempt at rendering a Kabir couplet into an English iambic pentameter couplet I found the task unmanageable. Then I realized that a few couplets could be transversed into an English iambic pentameter couplet but others seemed totally unmanageable. I made my next attempt with an octosyllabic line. I felt the task was manageable. Thus, the stanza-form adopted is of four lines—

second line rhyming with the fourth line and each line having four iambic feet. There are some exceptions when the line is not iambic but becomes trochaic. In this respect, my doctoral studies on Robert Frost helped me a lot. Frost in theory advocated and in his practice demonstrated that loose iambic lines have colloquial rhythm. Strict iambic becomes a sing-song which may be metrically correct but its touch with speech is lost. Kabir's couplets in the *Sakhi* have a colloquial rhythm. In regard to the stanza-form, I verified from the practice of other poets. I found that Keats in his "La Belle Dame Sans Merci" has similar form except that the last line is only of four syllables. Robert Frost in "A Record Stride" is of the same pattern:

> I touch my tongue to the shoes now,
> And unless my sense is at fault,
> On one I can taste Atlantic,
> On the other Pacific, salt.

In William Butler Yeats's poem "The Fiddler of Dooney" the same kind of stanza is used with extra unstressed syllable at the end of the first and third lines:

> When I play my fiddle at Dooney,
> Folk dance like a wave of the sea,
> My cousin is priest at Kilvarnet,
> My brother in Mocharabuiee.

I felt a couplet of Kabir finds its equivalent in the stanza-form adopted here.

In regard to rhyme as well the practice of English and American poets was kept in mind. In many stanzas the rhyme words are not phonetically exact. This kind of variation is justified by such critical terms as 'eye rhyme' 'slant rhyme' and so on.

It has to be frankly acknowledged that all the qualities of the original cannot be transversed. Alliteration, assonance, and pun in the original become the first casualties in translation. Meaning has been the main consideration so the best possible attempt is made to keep the meaning faithfully conveyed. A limited free play becomes unavoidable. In this connection, it is pertinent to quote Prakash Chander, the translator of *Flute and Bugle*: "the difficulty of rendering Urdu into English is sought usually *to be neutralised by limited free play with words and meanings even while staying anchored to the sense of original*" (Underlines mine) (Quoted from *Hindustan Times*, July 23, 1998).

Acknowledgments

I am grateful to my former colleague Dr. B.M. Gupta, Reader in Hindi, Radhe Hari Govt. Post-graduate College, Kashipur Distt. Udhamsingh Nagar who encouraged me for this work and suggested me what books I should have for going ahead with the work. I express my gratitude to several scholars of Hindi literature who encouraged me for going ahead with the work.

I am also grateful to my wife Mrs. Bindu Karki for keeping me encouraged in the entire duration of this work.

Contents

Contents

A Brief Biographical Sketch of Kabir

About Kabir's birth and parentage there is no unanimity among
the biographers of Kabir. On the basis of external and internal
sources there is near-agreement on certain facts. Kabir is said
to be born at a place called Lahartara in Kashi (the modern-
day Varanasi in U.P.) on the banks of the sacred river Ganges
on the full-moon day falling in between mid-May to mid-June
of the year 1398. A brahmin widow is said to be the mother
of Kabir. Because of social disgrace the brahmin widow cast the
new-born in a bush from where the weaver couple, Neema and
Neeru, picked up the new-born and adopted for bringing up.
Not long ago Neema and Neeru's forefathers had embraced
Islam. The weavers in general were poor and in terms of social
stratification they belonged to low caste and class. Neema and
Neeru could not afford the formal education of Kabir so they
initiated him to their trade of weaving. Kabir's own verse is
quoted for his lack of formal education:

> I did not touch ink and paper,
> Nor a pen in hand did I hold;
> Essence of Four-Ages wisdom
> By words of mouth I did unfold.

In the poetry of Kabir there is frequent use of imagery related
to weaving which gives proof of his trade of weaving.

Kabir is said to be the disciple of the famous *vaishnav* saint
Ramananda. Kabir was of low caste so it seems Ramananda did
not accept him initially. There is a tale that Kabir hid himself
on the stairs of a Kashi *ghat* (staired embankment for the
facility of bathers along the sacred river Ganges) from where
Ramananda used to pass to and fro for his dip-bath in the
Ganges. Ramananda's foot fell on Kabir. By way of mercy,
Ramananda is said to have accepted Kabir as his disciple. On

this point also there is no unanimity among the biographers as on Ramananda's death Kabir is said to be a lad of 13 years.

Once this fact is acknowledged that Kabir had no formal education, his powers of assimilation from varied sources were extraordinarily superb. The mass of learning that Kabir displays in his poetry might have its sources in Kabir's coming across men of learning of various religions, sects and schools. Kabir seems gifted with a sensitive ear, a retentive memory and a receptive mind. His acquisition and assimilation of knowledge and wisdom compares to Shakespeare's who too had 'little Latin and less Greek'. Though Kashi remained the centre of his activities, Kabir travelled far and wide. Seeing the mastery of different languages and dialects it is certain that he travelled extensively in the central and northern India. Keeping in view that journeys in those days were done on foot, especially by the poor, the travels of Kabir are astounding. Those travels were the sources of his knowledge, wisdom, experience and word-power—a truth come alive that 'travel is a form of education'.

In the life of Kabir the incidents related to Sheikh Taki are very famous. On the complaint of Sheikh Taki (a Muslim saint) Sikandar Lodi, the king of Muslim India, wanted to kill Kabir. An elephant with a mahaut was set to crush Kabir under its feet. The elephant instead of crushing Kabir to death is said to have run away with a roar. Next, Kabir was set to sink in the river with a weight of chains tied on him but Kabir is said to have a miraculous escape. The tale of Sikandar Lodi's atrocities became common among the biographers of Kabir. From Kabir's poetry treated as primary source it becomes clear that Kabir could not continue good relations with Sheikh Taki.

Kabir led a married life about which too there is not near-perfect unanimity among the biographers. Kabir's wife is said to be named Loiee. Some biographers say that his wife's name was Dhaniya which was later on changed to Ramjaniya. It is also said that he married twice—his first wife was ugly with evil signs and symptoms, the second was beautiful, loyal and devoted. This reference in Kabir's poetry as primary source is dismissed by modern critics making the plea that symbolic meaning of Kabir's verse lines cannot be taken literally. It is said he had two sons and two daughters. One of his sons was called Kamal who seems unworthy of Kabir's expectations.

Tatwajeewa, Bhaggodas, Jaggodas and Bijali Khan were Kabir's disciples and Raidas was a junior contemporary. Guru Nanak, the founder of Sikhism, was a contemporary of Kabir. He lived a life of more than a hundred years . The place called Maghar is associated with Kabir's birth and death. In contrast to the Hindu belief that one who dies in Kashi goes to heaven and one who dies at Maghar goes to hell, Kabir espoused Maghar where, according to some biographers, he died in 1518. "A beautiful legend", says Evelyn Underhill, "tells us that after his death his Mohammadan and Hindu disciples disputed the possession of his body; which the Mohammadans wished to bury, the Hindus to burn. As they argued together, Kabir appeared before them, and told them to lift the shroud and look at that which lay beneath. They did so, and found in the place of the corpse a heap of flowers, half of which were buried by Mohammadans at Maghar, and half carried by the Hindus to the holy city of Benares to be burned—fitting conclusion to a life which had made fragrant the most beautiful doctrines of two great creeds".

Introduction

Kabir: The Saint-Poet

The early twentieth century literary criticism of Hindi Literature was influenced by English literary criticism. Ram Chandra Shukla was a powerfully influential critic who opined that Kabir was a *social-reformer* and *not a poet* (I remember questions in examination papers were set to prove that Kabir was a social reformer and not a poet). At the beginning of the twentieth century I feel a great harm was done to Kabir. The powerful and influential critic Ram Chandra Shukla seems to have prejudiced readers to read Kabir in the way he liked. In order to set the things in proper perspective I.A. Richards is being quoted:

> Any Art which is infective, as he [Tolstoy] uses that word...is pure Art as opposed to modern or adulterated Art; but in deciding the full value of any work of Art we have to consider the nature of the experience communicated. The value of art contents is judged, according to Tolstoy, by the religious consciousness of the age. For Tolstoy the religious consciousness is the higher comprehension of the meaning of life, and this according to him, is the universal union of men with God and with another.... Culture, religion, instruction in some special senses, softening of the passions and the furtherance of good causes may be directly concerned in our judgements of the *poetic* values of experiences. Otherwise, as we shall see, the word 'poetic' becomes a useless sound.... The third point arises with regard to Dr. Bradley's position, that the consideration of ulterior ends, whether by the poet in the act of composing, or by the reader in the act of experiencing tends to lower poetic value. Here all depends upon *which are the ulterior ends in question* and what the kind of poetry.

It will not be denied that for some kinds of poetry the *intrusion* of certain ulterior ends may, and often does, lower their value; but there seem plainly to be other kinds of poetry in which its value as poetry definitely and directly depends upon the ulterior ends involved. Consider the Psalms, Isaiah, the New Testament, Dante, the *Pilgrim's Progress*, Rabelais, any really universal satire, Swift, Voltaire, Byron.

In all these cases the consideration of ulterior ends has been certainly essential to the act of composing. That needs no arguing; but equally this consideration of the ulterior ends involved is inevitable to the reader.... There is a kind of poetry into the judgements of which ulterior ends directly and essentially enter; a kind part of whose value is directly derivable from the value of the ends with which it is associated.... The separation of poetic experience from its place in life and its ulterior worths, involves a definite lop-sided-ness, narrowness, and its incompleteness in those who preach it sincerely.... It is impossible to divide a reader into so many men—an aesthetic man, an intellectual man, and so on. It cannot be done. In any genuine experience all these elements inevitably enter.

In the foregoing quotation, I.A. Richards seems to have concluded the controversy between 'poesie pure' and poetry that instructs and delights. In the present book, the basis of selection of couplets of the *Sakhi* for transcreation rests on Kabir's poetic merits. Poetry must stand on its own feet. It must have its permanence against the fleeting and the transitory. The question of permanence in literature is better understood by, what Matthew Arnold called, 'the real estimate' *vis-a-vis* the personal estimate and historical estimate. The real estimate necessarily leads to the consideration of Kabir as poet.

The first and foremost basis of selection of *Dohas* (Hindi couplets) from the *Sakhi* is Kabir's proverbial wisdom. (each couplet of Kabir is independent in meaning with a few exceptions where in one couplet questions are put forth and in succeeding couplet answers are given). Kabir gave them the name 'the witness'. Kabir's couplets imply what in the western

literature is called 'the didactic verses' or 'the moral verses'.
Kabir meant them the products of his own experience (much
like the 'essai' concept of Montaigne). Didactic is instructive
which is to impart instruction, advice, exhortation or some
doctrine of philosophy (the ulterior ends in the quotation
from I.A. Richards). The examples of the Sanskrit poet Bharthari
is a glaring example. Before Kabir, the *Gita* is didactic; the tales
of the *Hitopadesh* and *Panchtantra* are didactic. Some poets,
such as, Maluk Das, Dadu Dayal, Raidas and Rahim are didactic
poets.

Right from the primary to the graduate level, wherever Kabir's
poetry (mostly from the *Sakhi*) is prescribed for reading, a
number of Kabir's verses have become household quotes. Even
a common man is supposed to know the couplets which in
transcreation are:

> The company of the righteous
> Others sorrows doth mitigate;
> While company of the unrighteous
> Is grief for all the triad hours eight.

> No meditation equals truth,
> Equal to falsehood there's no sin;
> In whoever's heart lies the truth,
> Know it's that heart where God dwells in.

> Do today what thou'lt tomorrow,
> Do just now what thou'lt today,
> When wilt thou do many a task?
> In a moment Deluge will sway.

The second consideration for selection of *Dohas* rests on Kabir's
wonderful powers of analogy-finding in its multiple forms. This
analogy-finding trait, first of all, comes to light in the use of
similes. For Kabir, a righteous man is like a winnowing basket,
the victim of ill-company is like banana when briar's beside,
uncountable are desires like tree-leaves and sand-grains in the
Ganges, like the cat that watches the rat so Death waits on man

to lay seize, and, like the crane that seems meditate but pounces
on fish in wisdom immersed. In one of the couplets Kabir has
used a metaphor which is further illustrated by a simile:

Lotus leaves are the righteous men
In the midst of the world who home;
Alike a child's foster-mother
Who doesn't know the child as her own.

If we have a look at the greatest of world poets and even
philosophers we see that analogy-finding trait in its simplest
form of simile is widespread. The use of simile itself serves the
first purpose of poetry as it makes concrete what is abstract in
its idea or notion.

The analogy-finding trait of Kabir leads to a consideration
of Kabir's use of metaphor. The purpose of this introduction
is to rank Kabir in the great tradition of great poets of the east
and west. For this purpose to prepare a suitable background
of literary criticism seems essential. In literary criticism the
poet is regarded as a second creator. This is nowhere more
obviously true than in metaphors. The metaphor is conceived
as presiding alongwith music, at the very birth of speech, of
ideas and of human institutions. Primitive man thinks in sym-
bols, allegories and metaphors, combinations of these make
fable and myth. With the Schlegels, poetry, especially, meta-
phor is a perennial mother speech, a promise and vehicle of
future human institutions. When great and sensitive critics have
held metaphor in such high opinion, Kabir may be found in
the highest rank of poets.

Kabir's poetry abounds in metaphors. His metaphors based
on analogy partake of his intellectual virtues. It is the sign of
Kabir's genius that his use of metaphors implies an instinctive
similarity of dissimilars. For Coleridge, the imagination is "the
power by which one image or feeling is made to modify many
others and by a sort of fusion to force many into one... com-
bining many circumstances into one moment of thought that
ultimate end of human thought and human feeling, unity".
Metaphor shaped through imagination does not record pre-
existing similarities in things, rather, it is the linguistic means

by which Kabir brings together and fuses into a unity diverse thoughts and thereby re-form our perceptions of the world. For the sake of illustration, Kabir's use of 'stone', apart from its use as building material, for different metaphorical meanings may be taken up in a little detail:

In 'stone-made is this human body' stone is dust particles in geological processes and in metaphysical sense this human body is made of dust so of stone. Stone is used in the second sense 'stone made is the idol of god' 'stone' suggests sculpture, on the one hand, and, idol worship, on the other. Stone is used in the third sense when 'the boat is made of iron/which is heavily loaded with stones' when 'stones' suggest heaviness which metaphysically suggests heaviness of sins. In the fourth sense, stone suggests lack of sensitive receptivity as in

> It drizzled in graceful drizzles,
> On the stone fell showers of rain,
> The soil melted when it got watered
> But the stone showed no mark of change.

Similar to it, in the line 'too much reading has made thee stone', 'stone' suggests insensitivity to the divine message. Lastly, the universality of death appears to Kabir in the running mill where in 'between two blocks of stone/no single grain remains intact.' This illustration proves that Kabir does not record pre-existing similarities between the things or ideas, rather, Kabir makes us aware of new and fresh perceptions.

Elsewhere in Kabir there are brilliant uses of metaphor, such as, the body is town-in-fort which has five thieves and ten gates, human body is a pitcher, brahmin is the ass of the world who is loaded with pilgrimage, the world is a cell of soot, the guru is a burnisher of gold, maya is a hell-cat or a she-sinner or a three-fold tree or a prostitute, Kabir is screwpine haunted by a host of disciple-bees, wife of one but cuckolded by many this world is a polyandrous woman, and, so many others. Here is an extended metaphor:

> The wisdom-hurricane set in,
> And collapsed the wall of doubts,

    The maya-curtain flew away,
    And in heart love for God sprouts.

There is poetic richness when he with metaphors makes hyper-
bolic statements, such as:

    Let me make the whole earth my paper,
    And all the forest trees my pen
    Let me make ink of seven seas
    But Hari's glory I can't pen.

It is to the credit of Kabir that his use of metaphor is orna-
mental but at the same time his mind is actively and creatively
engaged in the forming of precepts and concepts and unifying
what is dissimilar or diverse. Kabir's metaphor has irreducible
meaning and a distinct cognitive content.

    The critics and expositors of Kabir's poetry seem to restrict
several beauties in his poetry by labelling them 'metaphors' or
'extended metaphors'. Many of Kabir's couplets are miniature
parables, fables, allegories and ironies. To term these classifi-
cations of subtler and finer nature simply as 'metaphor' is to
restrict their meanings and beauty. From the *Bible* the word
'parable' has come to be famous. Parable means saying one
thing and meaning another. *Oxford Universal Dictionary Illus-
trated* defines it as a "fictitious narrative usually of something
that might naturally occur by which moral or spiritual lessons
are typically set forth". Kabir has instinctive grasp of parable-
like metaphor. For example:

    The child threw and dashed into pieces
    The sugar loaf showing anger,
    He wept and in weeping state
    Went and met his beloved Father.

The meaning becomes clear when the child (son) is taken as
devotee, sugar-loaf as material possessions and beloved father
as God.

In a number of couplets Kabir has used fables in miniature. 'Fable' comes under the very broad category of metaphor because it too is saying one thing and meaning another. A fable is usually a short tale with animals in it. The verse

> Into the cave of mirrors
> The dog happened to make his race,
> In mirrors saw his own image
> So barked and died in barking state.

may serve as example. There are fable-like expressions, such as, 'old age dog in chase of youth hare', 'the fly is glued to jaggery' and many others. In Kabir's couplets there is recurrent use of 'swan' and 'crane'. It is clear that Kabir is not at literal level. The use of animals is by way of fable or symbol about which a brief discussion is a few pages ahead.

In English literature 'allegory' is very much celebrated. In Hindi, there is no clear-cut term or word for allegory. This too is placed in the category of extended metaphor. John Bunyan, the writer of the famous prose allegory the *Pilgrim's Progress*, said allegory to be a 'dark conceit'. In its Greek meaning it is speaking in other terms. Allegory rests on its chief element of personification of abstract virtues and vices. Kabir had an instinctive sense of allegory. The scope of a couplet is very brief but in that brevity too Kabir has displayed it wonderfully. In one couplet 'Wavering-Mind and Thievish-Heart/These two embarked on pilgrimage' personification is used. The verse

> On the horse of love, says Kabir,
> Awakened Mind, the rider, rode,
> And with his sword of wisdom hit
> Time's head and a pitched battle fought

may serve as example. There is another example:

> The cell of precious stones of wisdom
> Is locked with silence lock,
> Open it before the assayer
> With the key of honey-sweet talk.

A careful reading of the corpus "Of Maya" gives sufficiently clear hints that Maya is an abstraction but right from the ancient times of Sanskrit literature, the abstract Maya has personified form, so Kabir further personifies her as a hell-cat, a she-sinner, a prostitute, an enchantress and so on.

Sometimes Kabir's couplets fall in the category of 'irony' which too is a mode of saying one thing and meaning another. *Oxford Universal Dictionary Illustrated* defines 'irony' as a "figure of speech in which the intended meaning is the opposite of that expressed by the words used usually taking the form of sarcasm or ridicule in which laudatory expressions are used to imply condemnation or contempt". Here is an example:

> The holy tale the brahmin tells
> (Kabir says) is like boat of four;
> Assembled sit all the blind men,
> Wherever they like they do row.

Analogy-finding trait of Kabir makes an easy transition to his symbolism. Kabir is a symbolist and he might have agreed with Emerson's view "we are symbols and inhabit symbols". Baudelaire in French poetry is regarded as a great symbolist poet. His theoretical statements refer to his 'system of correspondences' which itself might have been suggested to him by Edgar Allan Poe's 'multiform combinations'. Baudelaire says:

> There is symbolic sense and every object in nature has its special connection with spiritual reality....
> Since sensuous data can have the expansion of infinite things, it follows that a desire, a regret, a thought—things of the mind can awaken a corresponding symbol in the world of imagination (and *vice versa*)... From the world of the senses the poet takes the material in which to forge for himself a symbol, what he asks of the world of the senses is that it gives him the means of expressing his soul.

In one verse Kabir has himself said:

> It's rare to come across a man
> With symbols able to conceive,
> When the ear is without perception
> Even the drum beat one may not perceive.

In the verse

> No sooner did the poacher see
> The quadrup'd than he ran for good;
> I happened to witness a wonder:
> The dead devouring the firewood

the poacher is metaphorical symbol of death and the beast he intends to hunt and kill is the pure, majestic soul free from worldly desires. It is in this sense that the poacher tries to escape rather than the beast. The statement is paradoxical. Soul does not die. The famous English poet John Donne suggests what Kabir means to say:

> One short sleep past, we wake eternally,
> And death shall be no more, death thou shalt die.

In another verse

> In fire ablaze the sea was burnt,
> The birds flew away in escape,
> The true guru had exhorted
> That burnt body doesn't germinate.

In symbolic interpretation, the sea is human body—the assemblage of desires—which is set ablaze by a true guru with the intense fire of wisdom. The birds symbolize humans who are enamoured of desires but with the wisdom they take shelter in the guru. Desires burnt with the fire of wisdom do not germinate again.

The complex system of Kabir's symbolism is often referred to as *ulatwamsis*, literally, reversed way of saying. In the tradition of English literature they may be called 'paradoxes'. So many objects of nature in Kabir's poetry have a system of symbolism.

For the sake of illustration, swan is used for majestic soul and crane for man in the grip of maya ready to grab the fish of material possessions so polluting the water. Diamond is the symbol of a true devotee. The exposition of Kabir's poetry sometimes becomes difficult because of the set of symbolism. When Kabir becomes highly metaphysical, his implied set of symbolism helps bring out the meaning. Not only in the imagery but in numbers also, Kabir has implied symbols. Literal meaning of couplets in the corpus "Of the Loyal Wife" and "Of the Loyal Wife sans Desire of Fruit" may not do justice to Kabir's richness in meaning if its suggestive and connotative nature is not taken into account.

The third consideration for selection of couplets from Kabir's *Sakhi* is rich imagery. Caroline Spurgeon's *Shakespeare's Imagery and What it Tells Us* seems to suggest that a similar study on Kabir's imagery be taken up. Similes and metaphors (in various forms) discussed above are part of Kabir's imagery but there is need of elaborating it at some length. Kabir's imagery is immensely rich. This might be the reason Kabir is regarded as a mystic. Elizabeth Drew's statement quoted here provides the right kind of background:

> The personality of the poet, which is the well-spring of his poetry, is fed by innumerable streams and channels of consciousness: by all that he has lived and suffered and enjoyed; all that he has observed and experienced by his senses; all that he has read of other men's creation and which has become part of his own being; all that he has read and speculated upon; his poetry will be a world created from all that he has known and felt and seen and heard and thought; and his image-making poetic faculty, his 'imagination', will blend together his memories and his immediate perceptions into a thousand varieties of shapes and associations of living loveliness and power.

What Elizabeth Drew theoretically says may be seen in application to Kabir. Evelyn Underhill in her introduction to Rabindranath Tagore's translation of 100 songs of Kabir writes, "all must be struck by the constant employment in them of imagery drawn from the common life, the universal experience". Kabir's imagery comprises

1. men with their activities of every trade and profession,
2. fauna and flora,
3. landscape and topographical features,
4. streams, rivers, seas and oceans,
5. huts, buildings, temples, mosques and palaces,
6. weather and climatic conditions,
7. market-places, buyers and sellers,
8. mythological gods, heroes and allusions to myths,
9. hell, purgatory and heaven,
10. supernatural beings and creatures,
11. weights and measures,
12. coins and coinage,
13. rare and precious stones,
14. tools, implements and weapons,
15. sleep and dream, and
16. human and animal actions.

In the all-pervading and wide-ranging imagery the main purpose is to seek analogy or comparison with the aim of bringing out his meaning and giving his message in crystal-clear limelight.

In 1912 in London, the Imagiste poets talked of visual image. Pound defined the image that makes "an emotional and intellectual complex in an instant of time". When it is the question of visual images Kabir has the gift, as in

> The love-lorn stands at the road edge,
> Runs when a passerby she sees,
> 'Just say a word about my Love,
> When will he come me to meet?'

The same kind of visual image is found in "with a big load tied on his back,/The traveller at road end stood". This visual image becomes suggestive of deeper meaning which may be brought out by quoting Christian of Bunyan's *Pilgrim's Progress*: "...I fear

that this burden that is upon my back will sink me lower than
the grave, and I shall fall into Tophet". In our common expe-
rience we see flies are attracted by sugar or jaggery. Jaggery in
heat and moisture becomes thick liquid. Flies in such a liquid
are pictured by Kabir:

> The fly is glued to jaggery
> Wherein all its wings are soaked;
> Clap thy hands and beat thy forehead!
> Alas! in the sweet it gets choked.

This example also shows that Kabir is not writing an image
poem with its surface meaning but he implies metaphysically
higher meaning as in this case howsoever worldly possessions
are condemned, a human being is attached to them and dies
in those material pursuits like the fly dying in liquid jaggery.

Not only this, in his use of imagery, Kabir shows the powers
of creating dramatic situations. A simple-looking line, such as,
Why dost thou shout, "I am hungry"/And let people listen to
thee?" the dramatic situation of the protagonist questioning
the passive listener becomes vivid and like the *in medias res*
device used by Shakespeare and Browning it becomes clear
that the talk between the protagonist and the passive listener
had been going on before the utterance was made. To illus-
trate it further in two similar images, "Seeing the gardener's
wife come,/Shout aloud the buds that are young" and "Seeing
the tree-feller come near,/The tree in terror starts to shake"
dramatic situations come alive. In a number of couplets the
created dramatic situations of (1) the speaker or protagonist,
(2) the passive listener, and (3) the tone of utterance, make
the meaning clear. In Kabir, there is image after image with
its infinite variety. The meaning enriches the image and the
image enriches the meaning.

The fourth consideration for selection of couplets from the
Sakhi is the theme of death that is recurrent in Kabir's poetry.
Carpe diem is a Latin phrase which means 'seize the day' or
'make the best of the present moment'. The phrase, what in
Christian poems and sermons, warns human beings to prepare

their bodies for death rather than their bodies for beds. The other Latin phrase *memento mori* means 'remember that thou shalt die' is also very famous. In Kabir's couplets of the *Sakhi* there is frequent use of death motif. Death is a universal feature and every literature has this theme in one way or the other. Shakespeare especially in his sonnets has rich expressions, such as, 'Nor shall Death brag thou wander'st in his shade', 'yet do thy worst, old Time: despite thy wrong', 'When I have seen by Time's fell hand defaced/The rich proud cost of outworn buried age', 'Against the wreckful siege of wreckful days,/When rocks impregnable are not so stout,/Nor gates of steel so strong, but Time decays', 'Death's second self that seals up all in rest', 'Death, that feeds on men' and 'Devouring Time, blunt thou the lion's paws' and so on. In the song "Fear No More the Heat of the Sun"

> Golden lads and girls all must
> As chimney-sweepers come to dust.

The same theme finds its famous expression in James Shirley, the lines of which are a quotable quote:

> Sceptre and crown,
> Must tumble down,
> And in the dust be equal made.

Carpe diem motif finds its expression in Robert Herrick when he wrote:

> Gather ye rose-buds,
> Old Time is still a-flying;
> And this same flower that smiles today
> Tomorrow will be dying.

In Thomas Gray this theme of death finds its marvellous expression in his Elegy's stanza:

> The boast of heraldry, the pomp of power,
> All that beauty all that wealth ever gave,

Await alike the inevitable hour,
The paths of glory lead but to the grave.

In Oriental poetry of Persia, Omar Khayyam strikes the same
note in such expressions as: 'the Bird of Time has but a little
way/To flutter— and the Bird is on the Wing', 'The Wine of
Life keeps oozing drop by drop,/The leaves of Life keep fall-
ing one by one', 'Tomorrow!—Why, Tomorrow I may be/Myself
with Yesterday's Sev'n thousand Years', 'We are no other than
a moving row/Of Magic Shadow-shapes that come and go'.
Two stanzas from Fitzgerald's translation of *Rubaiyat of Omar
Khayyam* are being quoted in full:

Ah, make the most of what we yet may spend,
Before we too into the Dust descend;
Dust into Dust, and under Dust to lie,
Sans Wine, sans Song, sans Singer, and sans End!

'Tis but a Tent where takes his one day's rest
A Sultan to the realm of Death addresst;
The Sultan rises, and the dark Ferrash
Strikes, and prepares it for another Guest.

The foregoing discussion on the *carpe diem* and *memento mori*
theme in foreign poets may serve as a foil to show Kabir's
poetry in a better way. There are superb and poetically rich
expressions of Kabir when he recurrently points out the uni-
versality and omnipotence of death and momentary nature of
human life, such as, 'man is food of Time/Who holds some
in lap and some in jaws', 'Death perches just over thy head/
As bridegroom under welcome gate', 'Today, tomorrow, or
within/A few days ends this mortal frame', 'Like the cat that
watches the rat/So Death waits on man to lay seize', 'All the
living beings are deers/For Time the mighty hunter's sake'
and 'This body's a water bubble/And takes not much of time
to fade'. One or two examples may be quoted in full:

Turn by turn and in their own turns
So many dear friends passed away;

> Now o human! it's thy turn
> Which is fast approaching each day.
>
> What rises (in the sky) doth set down,
> What blossoms that doth fade away,
> What's erected that doth collapse,
> What comes that has to go away.

Kabir's ingenuity is displayed in a number of ways in dozens of images—all rich and varied. So many couplets of the corpuses entitled "Of Portent", "Of Time/Death", "Of the Indivisible" and couplets included under the heading "Miscellaneous" are the best in exploring the theme of death and brevity of human life. Kabir may be called a pessimist but from the standpoint of his philosophy the span of life is short so a human should seize the day by devoting to God and singing his glories.

The fifth consideration for selection of Kabir's couplets for transcreation is Kabir's gift of satire. One of the famous critics of Kabir is Hazari Prasad Dwivedi, who says, "In Hindi till today no forceful satirist has been born...He [Kabir] had the weapon of satire for his revolution". Kabir was in rebellion against so many social and religious evils that were rampant in the society of those times and still prevalent though some five centuries have passed. Here a mention of Jesus Christ is desirable. As everybody knows Christianity was born in rebellion to the literal form of Moses' teachings rather than their spirit. Jesus Christ, time and again, openly rebuked and criticised the Sadducees and the Pharisees. In the *New Testament* Jesus Christ says, "you Sadducees and Pharisees, you clean the utensil from outside, inside of which there is dirt and filth". It seems great saints and prophets think alike in similar states of affairs. Much of Kabir's satire is directed against hypocrisy. Almost all the verses in the corpus called "Of (Simulative) Guise" have satirical vein. Kabir condemns a Jain hypocrite:

> Garbed as ascetic, Kabir says,
> But in actions of crime involved,
> Whose outward seems all righteousness
> But inside he is a big fraud.

In the times of Kabir, hundreds of men must have been roaming in the garbs of righteous men, fakirs and followers of various creeds and religious schools. Kabir directs his satire against them:

> Wearing the garb of a tiger,
> (The hypocrite) paces like sheep,
> He doth speak the tongue of the fox
> The dog tears him apart and eats.

The loose saffron gown worn by a man symbolizes devotion to God by renouncing worldly desires. But the reality is otherwise so Kabir sarcasts: 'wearing the wreath does not avail/If devotion doesn't follow pace', 'Wearing the wreath doesn't avail,/ Let the knot of thy heart be freed' and

> By cleanshaving a hundred times
> Thy head, why shouldst thou spoil thy hair?
> Why dost not cleanshave thy heart
> Which doth store many a desire?

One of the most known verses of Kabir is:

> By assembling gravels and stones
> The mosque has been built, on its top
> The mullah shouts cock-a-doodle do;
> Has God hearing perception lost?

In a similar vein, Kabir satirizes stone-worship of Hindus. With a spark of wit Kabir says, 'If God is realized by stone-worship/ Then let me worship a mountain". The idol worship of Hindus is hit by Kabir again and again as in:

> Stone-made is this human body,
> Stone-made is the idol of god,
> Stone-blind is the worshipper himself,
> So worship is not in God's accord.

Kabir was against false learning or pseudo-learning. In the days of Kabir, Brahmins were literate or educated (especially in

Kashi where Kabir passed most part of his life). One of the
famous couplets is:

> Reading book after book the world died
> But none a pundit could become;
> One who reads monosyllabic
> 'Love' a pundit he doth become.

In another couplet Kabir says, 'Do away with all thy reading/
And let thy books in waters float'. Brahmins who were learned
in the Scriptures were perpetuating life-less and meaningless
rituals. It might be in the vein of Juvenal, the Roman satirist,
Kabir condemns the brahmins wholesale: 'An ass's better than
a brahmin', 'Brahmin is the ass of the world/Who is loaded
with pilgrimage', 'The clown is today's brahmin-priest', 'The
brahmin sank... with his sacred thread's forceful load' and
'The pundit's manuscripts are alike/The knowledge of a par-
tridge'. The corpus "Of the Shrewd (Brahmin)" is mostly with
satire against the shrewdness and pseudo-learning of those
days.
    Kabir is wholesale condemner of pilgrimage. There are many
witty turns of expression that condemn pilgrimage:

> Pilgrimage is the venom tree
> Which's spread over age to age,
> Kabir has uprooted the tree,
> Why should a man this hemlock take?

In another verse Kabir says:

> Cold water bath led them to death
> For their pilgrimage those who went;
> So Kabir says in shouts aloud:
> 'Reborn as devils they repent'.

Among Muslims too, pilgrimage to Kaaba and Karbala (called
'Haz') is condemned:

> Devoid of contentment, O Sheikh!
> Why shouldst thou go for pilgrimage?
> Since whose hearts are not full of truth,
> For those men Allah nowhere is.

The verses of the corpus "Of the Musk Deer" tell that God is within so needless to find Him in pilgrim centres.

The sixth consideration for selection of Kabir's couplets is to highlight the wonderful power of rhetorics of Kabir. Rhetorics is the deliberate exploitation of eloquence for the most persuasive effect. The use of rhetorical art is displayed in so many ways for exploring the potentials of language. In the verse

> Where there's wisdom there's religion,
> Where there is falsehood there is sin,
> Where there's avarice there is Death,
> Where there's pardon there God dwells in

There is brilliant use of anophora in the repetition of 'where' and 'there'. In one couplet Kabir says, 'Heart's subjugated by the five' and to give it emphasis Kabir says' Heart does not the five subjugate'. Kabir wants to tell the simple truth that the men of righteousness are not common but they are rare. For this he uses the rhetorical device of three allusions in order to emphasize the conclusive statement:

> All woods are not of sandalwood,
> There aren't troops of the chivalrous,
> All the seas do not contain pearls,
> So worldwide (rare) are the righteous.

In the verse

> Who with footsteps measured the earth;
> Who could the sea split asunder;
> Who weighed mountain lifting in hands;
> Death snatched them and ate soon after.

Kabir has used three allusions to mythology by which the mythical tales come alive and with the death of heroes alluded the simple truth of Death's omnipotence is established. Such rhetorical devices are a common feature of Kabir's *Sakhi* couplets. Kabir had an instinctive grasp of what in the sixteenth century English prose was displayed by Lyly in his book *Euphues*.

In the beginning of this introduction the view of Ram Chandra Shukla was contradicted. But his views have validity in the sense that there are dozens and dozens of the *Sakhi* couplets which are repetitive in nature and sometimes flat and insipid. Many of such couplets might be interpolations by the succeeding disciples of Kabir (this is a matter of scholarly criticism). There are many excellent couplets left out in the present book—couplets which are highly philosophic, abstruse and specially concerned with Kabir's theory of "Endocrines". Further, there are many couplets in several corpuses which have lost much of their significance though they might have been relevant in Kabir's times.

By way of conclusion Kabir may be compared with later John Donne when he became the Dean of St. Paul and wrote devotional poetry and gave sermons. Seeing the classification of the couplets into some one hundred corpuses, Kabir may be compared with Bacon who said, 'I have taken all knowledge to be my province'. New criticism has popularized words, such as, 'paradox', 'tension', 'ambiguity', 'irony' and so many others. They seem to suggest that Kabir needs a fresh discovery. Six hundred years after Kabir's birth there is the realization that Kabir was not only of his age but he is of all the ages and he is not only of India but of the whole world.

साखी

1. गुरूदेव¹ कौ अंग²

सतगुर³ सैंवा न को सगा, सोधी⁴ सई न दाति।
हरिजी⁵ सवाँ न को हितू, हरिजन⁶ सई न जाति॥ (1)

पीछैं लागा जाइ था, लोक वेद⁷ के साथि।
आगैं वै सतगुर मिल्या, दीपक दीया हाथि॥ (2)

जाका गुरू भी अंधला, चेला खरा निरंध।
अंधा अंधा ठेलिया, दून्यूँ कूप पड़ंत॥ (3)

चौसठि दीवा जोइ करि, चौदह चंदा माँहिं।
तिहि घरि किसको चानिणौं, जिहँ घर गोबिन्द नाँहिं॥ (4)

माया दीपक नर पतंग भ्रमि-भ्रमि इवै पड़ंत।
कहै कबीर गुरू ग्यान थैं, एक आध उबरंत॥ (5)

कबीर सतगुर ना मिल्या, रही अधूरी सीख।
स्वाँग जती⁸ का पहरि कर, घरि घरि माँगै भीष॥ (6)

1. Of Guru the Deity

No kin equals a true guru,[1]
No donor equals a wise man,
No well-wisher's equal to God,
No caste is equal to God's men. (1)

Accustomed to go in the rear
Of the Scriptures' convention band;
Forward, I met a true guru
Who placed lamp of light in my hand. (2)

One whose guru's blind, stone blind
Is the disciple being taught,
The blind pushing ahead the blind, (3)
Into a well both of them fall.

Having searched (with) sixty-four lamps,
Amidst fourteen nights of the moon,[3]
In that home whom do you search for?
There Govind[4], the Lord, does not home. (4)

Deluded again and again,
Man-moth falls on the Maya[5]-flame,
With the guru's wisdom, says Kabir,
One or two manage to escape. (5)

One who couldn't have a true guru,
For him precept is incomplete;
The disciple in fakir's guise
Begs door to door (banters Kabir). (6)

2. सुमिरन र ग

दुख में सुमिरन[1] सब करै, सुख में करै न कोय।
जो सुख में सुमिरन करै, तौ दुख काहै को होय॥ (1)

कबीर सूता क्यां करै, उठि न रोवै दुक्ख।
जाका वासा गोर में, सो क्यूँ सोवे सुक्ख॥ (2)

कबीर सूता क्या करै, गुण गोविन्द[2] के गाइ।
तेरे सिर पर जम खड़ा, खरच कदे का खाइ॥ (3)

कबीर सूता क्या करै, सूताँ होइ अकाज।
ब्रह्मा का आसण खिस्या, सुनत काल की गाज॥ (4)

राम पियारा छाड़ि करि, करै आन का जाप।
बेस्वाँ केरा पूत ज्यूँ, कहै कौन सूँ बाप॥ (5)

लूटि सकै तो लूटियौ, राग नाम भंडार।
काल कंठ ते गहेगा, रूँधैं दसूँ दुवार॥ (6)

गुरू गोविंद दोनों खड़े, किसके लागों पाँय।
बलिहारी गुरू आपने, गोविंद दिया बताय॥ (7)

कबीर हरि के रूठते, गुरू के शरने जाय।
कहै कबीर गुरू रूठते, हरि नहिं होत सहाय॥ (8)

2. Of Remembering God

In sorrow all remember God,
But in happiness nobody;
Who remembers God in happiness
Why should ever sorrow there be? (1)

O how sad for him who's asleep!
In his grief he doesn't wake to weep,
One whose dwelling is in the grave,
In full ease he never can sleep. (2)

'Why art thou asleep?' says Kabir,
'Sing of God's glory, be awake!
Death doth stand just over thy head
For his daily ration's intake'. (3)

Why art thou asleep! says Kabir,
Greatly thy sleep may thee damage;
When Time maketh thundering sound
Even Brahma's[1] throne starts to shake. (4)

Leaving aside the beloved Ram
Who doth adore an alien god,
He is like the prostitute's son,
Whom to call his father knows not. (5)

Loot in as much as thou canst loot
Divine name of Ram in treasure;
God of Death will hold thee by throat
And throttle all thy ten apertures.[2] (6)

Guru and God stand side by side,
Whose feet should I touch and kowtow?
O Guru! I offer myself
At thy feet since God tells me so. (7)

When God's in the sulks, says Kabir,
To the guru for shelter goes,
But when guru is in the sulks
In no way the helper is God. (8)

कबीर ते नर अंध हैं, गुरू के कहते और।
हरि के रूठे ठौर है, गुरू रूठे नहिं ठौर॥ (9)

माला³ तो कर में फिरै, जीभ फिरें मुँह माँहिं।
मनुवा तौ चहुँ दिसि फिरै, यह तो सुमिरन नाँहिं॥ (10)

सतगुरू बड़े सर्राफ हैं, परखे खरा अरु खोट।
भवसागर⁴ ते काढ़ि के, राखैं अपनी ओट⁵॥ (11)

गुण गायै गुण न कटै, रटै न राम वियोग।
अह निसि हरि ध्यावै नहीं, क्यों पावै दुलभ जोग⁶॥ (12)

3. बिरह कौ अंग

बासुरि सुख नाँ रैणि सुख, नाँ सुख सुपिनै माँहि।
कबीर बिछुटया राम सूँ, नाँ सुख धूप न छाँह॥ (1)

बिरहनि¹ ऊभी पंथ सिरि, पंथी बूझै धाइ।
एक शब्द² कहि पीव का, कब रे मिलेंगे आइ॥ (2)

पूति पियारो पिता कौं, गौहनि लागा धाइ।
लोभ मिठाई हाथि दे, आपण गया भुलाइ॥ (3)

डारी खाँड़³ पटकि करि, अंतरि रोष उपाइ।
रोवत रोवत मिलि गया, पिता पियारे जाइ॥ (4)

Blind are those men who say guru,
Other than what he's, Kabir avers,
When God is in sulks there's room,
There's no room when guru's in sulks. (9)

Rosary doth rotate in hand,
Within mouth wags the tongue (to talk),
In four directions roams the mind—
This isn't the way to remember (God). (10)

True guru is a great jeweller
Who tests the genuine and the fake;
From the seas of this mundane world
He takes out gems for safety's sake. (11)

Singing attributes frees not from
Qualities[3]; cram Ram but forlorn;
Who don't adore God day and night,
How can they realize (the rare) God? (12)

3. Of Pain of Separation

Ease neither at day nor at night,
Even in dream there is no ease,
Ram-forsaken has ease neither
In shade nor in sun, says Kabir. (1)

The love-lorn stands at the road edge,
Runs when a passerby she sees,
'Just say a word about my Love,
When will He come me to meet?' (2)

The beloved son of his Father
Behind his Father walked along,
(Maya) placed greed-sweet in his hand
And he forgot Who was his own. (3)

The child threw and dashed into pieces
The sugar loaf begetting anger;
He wept and in weeping state
Went and met his beloved Father. (4)

परवति परवति मैं फिर्या, नैंन गँवाये रोइ।
सो बूटी पाऊँ नहीं, जातें जीवनि होइ॥ (5)

फाड़ि फुटोला धज करौं, कामलड़ी पहिराऊँ।
जिहि जिहि भेषाँ हरि मिलै, सोइ सोइ भेष कराऊँ॥ (6)

सुखिया सब संसार है, खावै और सोवै।
दुखिया दास कबीर है, जागै अरू रोवै॥ (7)

4. ग्यान बिरह¹ कौ अंग

हिरदा भीतर दौं² बलै, धूवाँ प्रगट न होइ।
जाकै लागी सो लखै, कै जिहि लाई सोइ॥ (१)

दौं लागी साइर जल्या, पंषी बैठे आइ।
दाधी देह न पालवै, सतगुर गया लगाइ॥ (2)

आहेड़ी³ दौं लाइयाँ, मृग⁴ पुकारैं रोइ।
जा वन में क्रीला करी, दाझत है वन सोइ॥ (3)

समंदर लागी आगि, नदियाँ जलि कोइया भईं।
देखि कबीरा जागि, मंछी⁵ रूषाँ चढ़ि गईं॥ (4)

From mountain to mountain I roamed,
Weeping too much my eyes turned sore;
That herb I was unable to trace
Which is life's base and vital core. (5)

Let me tear asunder silk clothes,
For a rough rug wear let me opt,
In whatever guise God's attained
That very guise I must adopt. (6)

Full of pleasure is the whole world
As it doth eat and it doth sleep,
But sad is devotee Kabir
Who doth keep awake and doth weep. (7)

4. Of Pain in Preceptive Enlightenment

Inside the heart there burns the fire
But nowhere the smoke is visible,
He only feels the burn who's burnt,
Or, he who did the fire enkindle. (1)

In fire ablaze the sea was burnt,
The birds flew away in escape,
The true guru had exhorted
That burnt body doesn't germinate. (2)

The poacher set forest ablaze,
Weeping aloud exclaims the deer:
'The same forest is burning now
Where I enjoyed sportful amour'. (3)

The sea caught fire and all rivers
Were burnt and to charcoal reduced,
Kabir witnessed it full awake
(And saw) the fish up the tree moved. (4)

5. परचा[1] कौ अंग

पाँणी ही तैं हिम भया, हिम ह्वै गया बिलाइ।
जो कुछ था सोई भवा, अब कछू न कह्या जाइ॥ (1)

पंषी[2] उड़ानी गगन कूँ, प्यंड[3] रह्या परदेस[4]।
पाँणी पीया चंच बिन, भूलि गया यहु देस॥ (2)

आया था संसार मैं, देषण को बहु रूप।
कहै कबीरा संत ही, पड़ि गया नजरि अनूप॥ (3)

जब मैं था तब हरि नहीं, अब हरि हैं मैं नाँहि।
सब औंधियारा मिटि गया, जब दीपक देख्या माँहि॥ (4)

जब मैं था तब हरि नहीं, अब हरि हैं मैं नाँहि।
कबिरा नगरी एक में, राजा दो न समाहिं॥ (5)

हम वासी वा देस को, जहाँ अविनाशी[5] की आन।
दुख सुख[6] कोई व्यापे नहीं, सब दिन एक समान॥ (6)

हम वासी उस देश[7] को, जहाँ बारा मास विलास।
प्रेम झरै बिलसैं कँवल, तेजपुंज परक़ास॥ (7)

कछु करनी, कछु करमगति, कछु पुरबीला लेख।
देखो भाग कबीर का, दोसत किया अलेख[8]॥ (8)

5. Of Communion (With God)

It is water which forms the snow,
Snow melts and becomes water again,
What it was ere, so it becomes,
To expatiate this there's no gain. (1)

The bird had its flight to the sky,
Its body lay in alien land,
It drank water without beak, and
Altogether forgot this land. (2)

I came to this world, says Kabir,
To behold manyness of form,
As saint I happened to witness
The unique in a single Form. (3)

When I was there, there was no God,
Now there's God and I'm non-existent,
All the darkness did melt away
When I saw in the light of lamp. (4)

With my ego there was no God,
Now there's God and I am effaced;
A single town, asserts Kabir,
Two kings doesn't accommodate. (5)

I'm the dweller of that land where
The Indestructible holds sway,
Delight and dole prevail not there,
Of equal measure is each day. (6)

I am the dweller of that land
Where's yearlong luxury's existence,
Where drizzles love, where lotus blooms,
Which's lighted by Mass of Radiance. (7)

Somewhat of deeds, somewhat of fate,
And somewhat of what's preordained,
See how fortunate is Kabir
The Invisible to befriend! (8)

लाली' मेरे लाल की, जित देखों तित लाल।
लाली देखन मैं गई, मैं भी भई निहाल॥ (9)

6. जणाँ' कौ अंग

भारी कहौं त बहु डरौं, हलका कहूँ तौ झूठ।
मैं का जाणौं राम कूँ, नैनूँ कबहुँ न दीठ॥ (1)

दीठा है तो कस कहूँ, कह्या न को पतियाइ।
हरि जैसा है तैसा रहौ, तू हरिषि हरिषि गुण गाइ॥ (2)

7. निहकर्मी पतिब्रता कौ अंग

दोजग' तो हम अंगिया, यह डर नाहीं मुझ।
भिस्त' न मेरे चाहिये, बाझ पियारे तुझ॥ (1)

जे वो एकै न जाँणियाँ, तौ जाँण्यॉ सब जाँण।
जे-वो एक न जाँणियाँ, तो सबही जाँण अजाँण॥ (2)

कबीर एक न जाँणियाँ, तौ बहु जाँण्यॉ क्या होइ।
एक तै तब होत हैं, सब तै एक न होइ॥ (3)

आसा एक जु राम की, दूजी आस निरास।
पाँणी माँहैं घर करें, तो भी मरै पियास॥ (4)

The rubric of my Ruby is
The more rubric the more I see;
I went so as to see the rubric
I too became full of ecstasy.[1] (9)

6. Of the Classic Ancient

I fear when I say He's ponderous,
It's untrue when I slight his weight,
What do I know of Ram? Because
My eyes saw Him not face to face. (1)

I have seen God but how should I say?
No one believes when it is said,
So let God remain as He is,
In sheer joy thou shouldst sing His grace. (2)

7. Of Loyal Wife Sans Desire of Fruit

I've accepted the nether world.
This is not the fear that lurks in me;
I am not in need of heaven,
O Lover! if it's without Thee. (1)

Though they know not the (divine) One,
They think everything they know;
If they know not the (divine) One,
What they know means nothing they know. (2)

Who knows not the One, says Kabir,
To know the many doth not avail,
The source of many is the One,
The many do not the One create. (3)

There is one hope and that's of Ram,
Hope in others is dejection.
In water itself one may home,
Of thirst he may die even then. (4)

कबीर कूता राम का, मुतिया मेरा नाउँ ।
गलै राम की जेबड़ी जित खैंचें तित जाउँ ॥ (5)

उस संम्रथ का दास हौं, कदे न होइ अकाज ।
पतिब्रता³ नाँगी रहै, तो उसही पुरिस कौ लाज ॥ (6)

8. चितावणी¹ कौ अंग

कबीर नौबति² आपणीं, दिन दस लेहु बजाइ ।
ए पुर पट्टन³ ए गली, बहरि न देखै आइ ॥ (1)

सातों सबद जु बाजते, घरि घरि होते राग ।
ते मंदिर⁴ खाली पड़े, बैसण लागे काग ॥ (2)

कबीर पटण कारिवाँ, पंच चोर दस द्वार ।
जम राणों गढ़ भेलिसी, सुमिरि लै करतार ॥ (3)

कबीर कहा गरबियो ऊँचे देखि अवास ।
काल्हि परयूँ भौं लेटणाँ, ऊपरि जामें घास ॥ (4)

कबीर कहा गरबियो, देही देखि सुरंग ।
बीछड़िया मिलिबौ नहीं, ज्यूँ काँचली भुवंग ॥ (5)

कबीर कहा गरबियो, इस जीवन की आस ।
टेसू⁵ फूले दिवस चारि, खंखर भये पलास ॥ (6)

'I'm the dog of Ram', says Kabir,
'Salvation-seeker I'm eclept,
Ram's chain is tied around my neck,
I go wherever He doth lead.' (5)

I'm devotee of Omnipotent,
So not to suffer loss or pain,
If the loyal wife is naked,
It's not her but her husband's shame. (6)

8. Of Portent

In pompous splendour of ten days
Beat thy kettle-drum, says Kabir,
Alas! this town and this alley!
Thou wilt not come again to see. (1)

If all the seven[1] notes did sing
Home to home music would burst forth,
But ah! empty lie the houses
And crows make cacophanous note. (2)

This body is a town-in-fort
Which has five thieves and ten gates,
Yama[2], the king, will seize the fort,
So remember God, Kabir says. (3)

Why shouldst thou be proud, says Kabir,
Seeing high-rise buildings to dwell,
Tomorrow they will lie down in dust
Over which grass will grow and swell. (4)

Why shouldst thou be proud, says Kabir,
Seeing thy body rich in complexion,
Separat'd once no reunion,
Similar to snake's cast off skin. (5)

Why shouldst thou be proud, says Kabir,
In cherishing hope of this life?
The *butae frandosa* flower
Has four-day span, then fades and dries. (6)

कबीर कहा गरबियो, काल⁶ गहै कर केस।
नाँ जाणौं कहाँ मारिसी, कै घरि कै परदेस॥ (7)

यहु ऐसा संसार है, जैसा सैबल⁷ फूल।
दिन दस के व्यौहार कौं, झूठै रंगि न भूल॥ (8)

हाड़ जरै ज्यूँ लाकड़ी, केस जलैं ज्यूँ घास।
सब तन जलता देखि करि, भया कबीर उदास॥ (9)

कबीर मंदिर ढहि पड़या, सेन्ट⁸ भई सैवार⁹।
कोई चेजारा¹⁰ चिणि गयो, मिल्या न दूजी बार॥ (10)

कबीर देवल ढहि पड़या, ईंट भई सैंवार।
करि चेजारा सौं प्रीतड़ी, ज्यों ढहै न दूजी बार॥ (11)

कबीर मंदिर लाष¹¹ का, जड़िया हीरें लालि।
दिवस चारि का पेषणाँ, बिनस जाइगा कान्हि॥ (12)

कबीर धूलि सकेलि करि, पुड़ी ज बाँधी एह।
दिवस चारि का पेषणाँ, अंत षेह का षेह¹²॥ (13)

कबीर सुपनै रैनि कै, उघड़ि आये नैंन।
जीव पड़या बहु लूटि मैं, जागै तो लैंन न दैंण॥ (14)

कहा कियो हम आइ करि, कहा करेंगें जाइ।
इत के भए न उत के, चाले मूल गँवाइ॥ (15)

Why shouldst thou be proud, says Kabir,
Time doth hold thy hair in His hands;
No one knows where He will kill thee
At thy home or in foreign lands. (7)

This world is in the likeness of
Flowers of red silk cotton tree,
In a ten-day festivity,
In false colours thou shouldst not be. (8)

(On the pyre) bones burn as fuelwood,
And hair burns as dry grass and weeds,
Seeing the entire body burning
Pensively sad becomes Kabir. (9)

This house has collapsed, says Kabir,
And all its bricks reduced to weeds,
Some Artisan had it erected,
Second time Who didn't come to meet. (10)

This house has collapsed, says Kabir,
And all its bricks reduced to weeds;
Grow thy love for the Artisan,
Second time collapse it mayn't meet. (11)

Of lakhs is this house, says Kabir,
Studded with diamonds and rubies,
For four-day span it is in sight,
Tomorrow its ruin it will meet. (12)

Assembling dust, opines Kabir,
This body's in paper-fold bound,
For four-day span it is in sight,
The end: dust mixes in dusty ground. (13)

In nocturnal dreams, says Kabir,
When broad open eyes are awake,
Human is lost in loot wholesole,
When awake there's no give and take. (14)

What did I do by coming here?
What shall I do when I depart?
Neither of this nor of the other;
Worst, with my capital I part. (15)

कबीर हरि की भगति बिन ध्रिगि[13] जीमण संसार।
धूवाँ केरा धौलहर[14], जात न लागै बार॥ (16)

मनिषा जनम दुलभ है, देह न बारंबार।
तरवर थैं फल झड़ि पड़या, बहुरि न लागे डार॥ (17)

यह तनु काचा कुम्भ है, चोट चहूँ दिस खाइ।
एक राम के नाँव बिन, जदि तदि प्रलै जाइ॥ (18)

यह तन काचा कुंभ है, लियाँ फिरै था साथि।
ढबका लागा फुटि गया, कछू न आया हाथि॥ (19)

खम्भा एक गइंद दोइ, क्यूँ करि बंधसि बारि।
मानि[15] करै तो पीव नहीं, पीव तौ मानि निवारि॥ (20)

दुनियाँ भाँडा दुख का, भरी मुहाँमुँह भूष।
अदया अलह राम की, कुरलै ऊँणी कूष॥ (21)

मैं मैं बड़ी बलाइ[16] है, सकै तो निकसी भाजि।
कब लग राखों हे सखी, रूई पलेटी आगि॥ (22)

कबीर नाब जरजरी, कूड़े खेवनहार।
हलके हलके तिरि गए, बूड़े तिनि सिर भार॥ (23)

पाँच पहर धंधे गया, तीन पहर रहा सोइ।
एक पहर हरि ना जप्यो, मुक्त कहाँ ते होइ॥ (24)

Without adoration of God,
Phew! this worldly life of disdain;
Like a high-rise palace of smoke
To melt in air no time doth take. (16)

It is rare to have human life,
This body isn't again and again
The fruit fallen down from the tree,
Does not stick to the branch again. (17)

This body is a brittle pitcher
From four directions which is hit,
Without the canoe of Ram's name
Deluges too oft will drift it. (18)

Thy body was a brittle pitcher
Which thou used to carry with thee,
It got a hit and soon broke down,
And thou didst find thy hands empty. (19)

There's one post but elephants two,
How can two together be tied?
If thou keepst pride, God is out,
If thou dost keep God, quit thy pride. (20)

This world is a pot of sorrow
Which's full of hunger to the brim,
Devoid of Ram's mercy, humans
Lie smug in spider's web they spin. (21)

Fiend lies in selfish I and I,
If thou canst, say to it 'avaunt',
O my friend! how far canst thou keep
The cotton that is in fire caught? (22)

Worn out is this boat, says Kabir,
Decrepit are who row the boat,
They could float who were light in weight,
But sank who on their heads had load. (23)

Five times triad³ hours spent in business,
And three times triad hours lost in sleep,
No triad hours for God's adoration,
So salvation's beyond thy reach. (24)

9. मन कौ अंग

मन¹ के मते न चालिये, छाड़ि जीव² की बाँणि।
ताकू केरे सूत ज्यूँ उलटि अपूठा आँणि॥ (1)

मन जाँणे सब बात, जाणत ही औगुन करै।
काहे की कुसलात³, कर दीपक कूँवैं पड़ै॥ (2)

हृदये भीतरि आरसी, मुख देषणाँ न जाइ।
मुख तौ तौपरि देखिए, जे मन की दुविधा जाइ॥ (3)

पाँणी ही तैं पातला, धूवाँ ही तैं क्षीण।
पवना बेगि उतावला, सो दोषत कबीरे कीन्ह॥ (4)

कबीर मन गाफिल भया, सुमिरन लागै नाहँ।
घणी सहैगा सासनाँ, जम⁴ की दरगह माहँ॥ (5)

कागद केरी नाँव री, पाँणी केरी गंग।
कहै कबीर कैसे तिरूँ, पंच कुसंगी⁵ संग॥ (6)

कबीर मन पंषी भया, बहुतक चढ़या अकास।
उहाँ ही तैं गिरि पड़या, मन माया के पास॥ (7)

भगति दुवारा सँकड़ा, राई दसवें भाइ।
मन तो मैंगल⁶ ह्वै रह्यो, क्यूँ करि सकै समाइ॥ (8)

9. Of Heart (Full of Desires)

Act not on dictates of thy heart,
And quit thy habit basely human,
Alike the yarn in a bobbin
Winds backward open when it's spun. (1)

Man's heart is in know of all things,
But knowingly in evil he rolls,
Not to talk of his well-be'ng, since
Lamp in hand into a well falls. (2)

There's mirror inside the heart,
But the human can't see his face;
Look at thy face mirrored upon
When melt 'way the doubts of ill-grace. (3)

Kabir has befriended that One
Who's much more fluid than water,
Very much feebler than smoke is;
And compared to wind's speed much faster. (4)

Full careless has become this heart,
So on prayers doesn't concentrate;
Tortuous blows of hammer it'll bear
When in the court of Yama's state. (5)

In the waters of the Ganges
My body is a paper boat,
Five bad companions[1] that I keep
(Ponders Kabir) how should I float? (6)

This heart is a bird, says Kabir,
That in the sky soars high and higher,
Therefrom it happens to fall down
Near the illusion of desire. (7)
The door to devotion is narrow
Which's a tenth part of a mustard;
How can the door accommodate
This heart-elephant run amuck? (8)

करता था तौ क्यूँ रह्या, अब करि क्यूँ पछताइ।
बोवे पेड़ बबूल का, अंब कहाँ तै खाइ॥ (9)

10. सूषिम[1] मारग कौ अंग

कौण देस कहाँ आइयाँ, कहु क्यूँ जाण्याँ जाइ।
उहु मार्ग पावै नहीं, भूलि पड़े इस माँहि॥ (1)

उतीथें कोई न आबई, जाँकू बूझौं धाइ।
इतथें सबै पठाइये, भार लदाइ लदाइ॥ (2)

जहाँ न चींटी चढ़ि सकें, राई ना ठहराइ।
मन पवन का गमि नहीं, तहाँ पहूँचे जाइ॥ (3)

11. सूषिम जनम[1] कौ अंग

प्राणपिंड को तजि चलें, मूवाँ कहै सब कोई।
जीव छताँ जाँमैं, मरै, सूषिम लखै न कोइ॥ (1)

12. माया[1] कौ अंग

जग हटबाड़ा स्वाद ठग, माया बेसाँ लाइ।
रामचरन नीकाँ गही, जिनि जाइ जनम ठगाइ॥ (1)

Why didst thou do thou wert used to?
Having done why repentance now?
From where canst thou a mango eat?
When thou didst an acacia grow. (9)

10. Of Subtle Ways

Which land was thine? Where hast thou come?
Where thou art destined? Thou knowst not;
Path to that land thou canst not find,
Here amidst this world strayed and lost. (1)

Thitherfrom nobody returns
Whom to ask I may haste to 'pproach,
All are dispatched hitherfrom, who
With them carry load over load. (2)

Where even an ant can't ascend,
Where tarries not the mustard seed,
Where mind-wind cannot approach,
Thither Kabir happens to accede. (3)

11. Of Subtle Birth

The soul departs from the body,
People around declare him dead;
Births and deaths frequent men who live
But no one knows the subtle fact. (1)

12. Of Maya

The world is a market-enclosure
Where gust-cheats set maya-courtesans,
Those who adhere fast to Ram's feet
Being cheated life-long they shun. (1)

कबीर माया पापणी, फंध ले बैठि हाटि।
सब जग तो फंधै पड़या, गया कबीरा काटि॥ (2)

कबीर माया मोहनी, जैसी मीठि खाँड़।
सतगुरू की कृपा भई, नहीं तो करती भाँड़॥ (3)

माया तरवर त्रिविध का, साखा दुख संताप।
सीतलता सुपिनै नहीं, फलि फीको तनि ताप॥ (4)

कबीर माया ढाकणीं, सब किसहीं कौं खाइ।
दाँत उपाणौं पापणीं, जे संतों नेड़ी जाइ॥ (5)

त्रिषणाँ सीचीं नाँ बुझें, दिन दिन बढ़ती जाइ।
जवासा के फूल ज्यूँ, घण मेहाँ कुम्हिलाइ॥ (6)

नलनी सायर घर किया, दौ लागी बहुतेणि।
जल ही माँहैं जलि मुई, पूरब जनम लिषेणि॥ (7)

माया छाया एक सी, बिरला जाने कोय।
भगता के पाछे फिरै, सनमुख आगे होय॥ (8)

माया की झल जग जल्या, कनक काँमणी² लागि।
कहु धौं किहि विधि राखिये, रूई लपेटी आगि॥ (9)

आँधी आई ज्ञान की, ढही भरम की भीति।
माया टाटी उड़ि गई, लगी नाम सौं प्रीति॥ (10)

Maya's she-sinner, says Kabir,
With noose sits in the market place,
Trapped in her noose is the whole world
But Kabir has cut down the same. (2)

Maya's enchantress, says Kabir,
Alike sweet sugar (enchants flies),
The true guru has been kind enough,
Ruin she would have brought otherwise. (3)

Maya is a tree of the Triple[1],
Whose branches are sorrow and pain;
Coolness from it is undreamt of,
Body with heat and fruits sans taste. (4)

Maya is hell-cat, says Kabir,
That eats everyone and each,
If she ever go near the saints
Let me uproot the sinner's teeth. (5)

Thirst doesn't quench by taking water,
Rather day by day doth increase,
Much like the chiranium flower
In too much of rain doth evanesce. (6)

Lotus opts to dwell in sea water
Where too it doth face burning heat,
In water itself dies of burns,
Destined so by former life's deed. (7)

Maya and shadow are alike,
About it rarely someone knows,
Both are frontward of run-of-the-mill,
Behind devotee each one goes. (8)

The world is burnt with maya's heat
In beloved-gold's arms embraced,
How far and what way can one keep
The cotton when in fir emblazed? (9)

The wisdom-hurricane set in
And collapsed the wall-of-doubts,
The Maya-curtain flew away,
And in heart love for God sprouts. (10)

कबिरा माया बेसवा, दोनों की एक जात।
आवत को आदर करें, जात न बूझै बात॥ (11)

बुगली³ नीर बिटालिया, सायर⁴ चढ़या कलंक।
और पखेरू पी गए, हंस⁵ न बौवै चंच॥ (12)

13. चाणक¹ कौ अंग

स्वामी हूँणाँ सोहरा, दोद्धा हूँणाँ दास॥
गादर आँणी ऊन कूँ, बाँधी चरैं कपास॥ (1)

चारिउ वेद पढ़ाइ करि, हरि सूँ न लाया हेत।
बालि कबीरा ले गया, पंडित² ढूँढे खेत॥ (2)

ब्राह्मण गुरू जगत का, साधू का गुरू नाँहि।
उरझि पुरझि करि मरि रह्या, चारौं वेदाँ माहिं॥ (3)

चतुराई सूवै पढ़ी, सोई पंजर माँहिं।
फिरि प्रमोधै आन कौं, आपण समझे नाँहिं॥ (4)

तारा मंडल बैसि करि, चंद बड़ाई खाइ।
उदै भया जब सूर का, स्यूँ तारा छिप जाइ॥ (5)

पंडित केरी पोथियाँ, ज्यों तीतर का ज्ञान।
औरन शकुन बतावहीं, अपना फंद न जान॥ (6)

Maya's a harlot, says Kabir,
Both of them belong to one caste,
For one who comes in, they welcome,
But one who goes out, they disregard. (11)

The she-crane defiled the water,
The sea bore the pollutants heap,
All other birds drank that water,
The swan didn't even dip its beak. (12)

13. Of the Shrewd (Brahmin)

It's easy to be a master
But difficult to be a slave,
For the sake of wool sheep was reared,
Tethered, it doth the cotton graze. (1)

(The pundit) read the Four Vedas
But for God didn't grow any love;
Kabir took away ears of grain,
Pundits in crop-field make a search. (2)

The brahmin is the world's guru,
Guru of the righteous he's not,
Entangled in the tangle of
The Four Vedas he is dead-lost. (3)

Cunningness did the parrot learn,
Even then it's inside the cage;
To all and sundry it exhorts,
To comprehend itself doth fail. (4)

Seated in the midst of the stars
The moon enjoys a lot of praise,
No sooner doth the sun rise, then,
Together with stars, it doth fade. (5)

The pundit's manuscripts are alike
The knowledge of a partridge,
To others doth tell good omen,
Of its own noose lacks the knowledge. (6)

चतुराई क्या कीजिये, जो नहिं शब्द समाय।
कोटिक गुन सुगना पढ़ै, अंत बिलाई खाय॥ (7)

पंडित और मसालची³, दोनों सूझै नाहिं।
औरन को करें चाँदना, आप अंधेरा माँहि॥ (8)

पढ़ि पढ़ि तो पत्थर भया, लिखि लिखि भया जो ईंट।
कबिरा अन्तर प्रेम की, लगी न एको छींट॥ (9)

पढ़ि पढ़ि तो पत्थर भया, लिखि लिखि भया जो चौर।
जिस पढ़ते साहब मिलै, तो पढ़ना कछु और॥ (10)

ब्राह्मण गदहा जगत का, तीरथ लादा जाय।
यजमान⁴ कहै मैं पुनि किया, वह मिहनत का खाय॥ (11)

ब्राह्मण ते गदहा भला, आन देव⁵ ते कुत्ता।
मुलनाते मुरगा भला, शहर जगावे सुत्ता॥ (12)

कबिरा ब्राह्मण बूड़िया, जनेऊ⁶ केरे जोरि।
लख चौरासी⁷ माँगि लई, पारब्रह्म सौ तोरि॥ (13)

कलि का ब्राह्मण मसखरा, ताहि न दीजै दान।
कटुंब सहित नरकै चला, साथ लिया यजमान॥ (14)

Oh! what use is the cunningness?
Which doesn't the Word[1] assimilate,
Crores of hymns the parrot repeats
But at last is eaten by cat. (7)

The pundit and the torch-bearer-
Either of two in darkness gropes,
To others he doth give the light
But he himself in darkness goes. (8)

Too much reading has made thee stone,
Too much writing has made thee brick,
In the heart of heart no wetness
Of love was found, Kabir doth think. (9)

Too much reading has made thee stone,
Too much writing has made thee thief;
That reading is altogether
Diff'rent which to the Saheb[2] leads. (10)

The brahmin is the world's ass
Who is burdened with pilgrimage;
The client[3] says, 'I did acts of goodness',
The brahmin has his labour's wage. (11)

An ass's better than a brahmin,
A dog's better than alien god;
Awakening a sleeping town
Much better proves a crowing cock. (12)

The brahmin sank, so Kabir says,
With his sacred thread's[4] forceful load,
He asked for eighty-four[5] (births)
Breaking off from Transcendental God. (13)

The *kalyug's*[6] brahmin is a clown
So to him ought not to donate,
With his family he's hellward bound,
Alongwith him his client doth take. (14)

14. करणीं बिना कथनी कौ अंग

कथणी कथी तो क्या भया, जे करणीं नाँ ठहराइ।
कालबूत' के कोट ज्यूँ, देषत ही ढहि जाइ॥ (1)

जैसी मुष तैं नीकसै, तैसी चालैं नाहिं।
मानिष नहीं ते स्वान गति, बाँध्या जमपुर जाँहिं॥ (2)

कथनी मीठी खाँड सी, करनी विष की लोय।
कथनी कथि करनी करै, विष से अमृत होय॥ (3)

15. कथनी बिना करणीं कौ अंग

कबिरा पढ़िबा दूरी करि, पुस्तक दे बहाइ।
बाँवन आषिर सोधि करि, रैं ममैं चित लाइ॥ (1)

पोथी पढ़ि-पढ़ि जग मुवा, पंडित भया न कोइ।
एकै आषिर पींव का, पढ़ै सु पंडित होइ॥ (2)

16. कामी नर व काम कौ अंग

काँमणि काली नागणीं तीन्यूँ लोक मँझारि।
राम सनेही ऊबरैं, बिषई खायें झारि॥ (1)

14. Of Deeds Sans Words

Mere words said has no use at all
If deeds do not them justify,
Alike the walls in scaffolding
Collapse sooner than we descry. (1)

If thy stepping is not in tune with
What thou dost in words articulate,
Thou meetst fate of dog not of man,
Bound in noose thou goeth to hell straight. (2)

Mere words uttered is sweet sugar,
Deed is a lump of poison dough;
If deeds are close on heel of words
From poison it transforms to nectar. (3)

15. Of Words Sans Deeds

Do away with all thy reading
And let thy books in waters float,
Thou hast learnt fifty-two alphabets,[1]
Now concentrate thy mind on God. (1)

Reading books and books the world died,
But none a pundit could become,
One who reads monosyllabic
'Love' a pundit he doth become. (2)

16. Of Lusty Man and Of Lust

In the three worlds[1] the aphrodisian—
The black-she-serpent[2]—is ubique,
Ram-devotees manage escape,
But stings those who're sensually weak. (1)

पर नारी पर सुंदरी, बिरला बंचै कोई।
खाताँ मीठी खाड़ सी, अंति काल बिष होई॥ (2)

काँमणि भीनी षाँणिं की, जे छेड़ौं तौ खाइ।
जे हरि चरणाँ राचियाँ, तिनके निकट न जाइ॥ (3)

पर नारी को राचणों, औगुण है गुण नाँहि।
षार समंद मैं मंझला, केता बहि बहि जाँहिं॥ (4)

कामी का गुरू कामिनी, लोभी का गुरू दाम।
कबिरा का गुरू सन्त है, संतन का गुरू राम॥ (5)

पर नारी पैनी छुरी, मति कोई लावो अंग।
रावण के दश सिर गये, परनारी के संग॥ (6)

पर नारी के राचने, साधो नरकै जाय।
यम तिनको छोड़ै नहीं, कोटिन करै उपाय॥ (7)

भगति बिगाड़ी कामियाँ, इन्द्री केरे स्वादि।
हीरा खोया हाथ थे, जनम गँवाया बादि॥ (8)

17. साँच कौ अंग

कबीर पूँजी साह[1] की, तू जिनि खोवै ष्वार।
खरी बिगूचनि होइगी, लेखा[2] देती बार॥ (1)

Rare it is to escape from charms
Of other's beautiful woman,
White eating she's sweet like molasses,
But at last turns into poison. (2)

The aphrodision is a bee
In a beehive, if vexed it stings,
Those who are enamoured of God
She dare not ever go near them. (3)

To be enamoured of other's wife
Has vices and no qualities,
Like fish ill-placed in salty sea
Goes on floating ill-at-ease. (4)

The lewd's guru's the aphrodisian,
Money is the greedy's guru,
Kabir's guru is who's a saint,
Of the saints Ram is the guru. (5)

Other's wife is a sharp-edged dagger,
So no one ought to embrace her;
Ravana[3] lost all his ten heads
While with the wife of the other. (6)

Being enamoured of other's wife,
The righteous too are in hell placed,
God of Death does not spare them
Though crores of endeavours they make. (7)

The lusty doth spoil devotion,
For the sake of his sensual taste,
First, he drops diamond from his hands,
Later on, his life he lays waste. (8)

17. Of Truth

This body is the capital
Of God-king, desecrate it not,
Much embarrassed thou wilt feel
When thou presentst account[1] to God. (1)

सेष सबूरी बाहिरा, क्या हज कावै जाइ।
जिनकी दिल स्यावति नहीं, तिनको कहाँ खुदाइ॥ (2)

कबीर जिनि जिनि जाणियाँ, करता केवल सार।
सो प्राणी काहै चलै, झूठै जग की लार॥ (3)

साँच बराबर तप नहीं, झूठ बराबर पाप।
जाके हृदय साँच है, ताके हृदये आप॥ (4)

साँचै कोइ न पतीजई, झूठे जग पतियाय।
गली गली गोरस फिरे, मदिरा बैठि बिकाय॥ (5)

साँच कहै तो मारि है, यह तुरकानी जोर।
बात कहूँ परलोक की, करिके पकरै चोर॥ (6)

पापी पूजा बैसि करि, भखै मांस मद होइ।
तिनकी दष्या मुक्ति नहीं, कोटि नरक फल होइ॥ (7)

जो तू साँचा बानिया, साँची हाट लगाय।
अन्दर झाड़ू देइके, कूरा दूर बहाय॥ (8)

18. भ्रमविधौंसण[1] कौ अंग

पाँहण केरा पूतला, करि पूजैं करतार।
इही भरोसे जे रहे, तू बूड़े काली धार॥ (1)

Devoid of contentment, O Sheikh!
Why shouldst thou go for pilgrimage?
Since whose hearts are not full of truth,
For those men Allah nowhere is. (2)

Whoever knows the Creator is
The only essence, Kabir says,
Then why should human traverse in
The much beaten false worldly ways? (3)

No meditation equals truth,
Equal to falsehood there's no sin;
In whoever's heart lies the truth,
Know it's that heart where God dwells in. (4)

Nobody believes in the truth,
All the world believes in the false,
The milkman peddles street to street
But liquor sells seated in stalls. (5)

If I speak the truth, the Muslim
Manhandles me and doth me beat,
I talk of the world that's beyond,
He arrests me and brands me thief. (6)

Sinful is the *vaishya's*[2] prayer,
Who doth drink liquor and eat flesh,
His state is not worth salvation—
He's fated to go crores of hells. (7)

If thou art a tradesman of Truth
Hold a market for Truth's exchange,
By grooming well within thyself,
Cast far away thy own garbage. (8)

18. Of End of Fallacy

An effigy sculptured in stone
People worship treating as Creator;
Those who rest contented with it
Sink in swift tide of black river. (1)

काजल केरी कोठरी, मसिके कर्म कपाट।
पाहनि बोई पृथमी, पंडित पाड़ी बाट॥ (2)

पाहिन कूँका पूजिये, जे जनम न देई जाब।
आँधा नर आसामुषी, यौं ही खोवै आब॥ (3)

तीरथ त सब बेलड़ी, सब जग मेल्या छाइ।
कबीर मूल निकंदिया, कौण हलाहल खाइ॥ (4)

कबिरा दुनिया देहुरे, सीस नवाँवण जाय।
हिरदा माँही हरि बसै, तू ताही लौलाय॥ (5)

पाहन पूजै हरि मिलै, तो मैं पूजूँ पहार।
ताते यह चाकी भली, पीसि खाय संसार॥ (6)

पाथर ही का देहरा, पाथर ही का देव।
पूजन हारा आँधरा, क्यों करि मानै सेब॥ (7)

काँकर पाथर जोरि के, मसजिद लइ चुनाय।
ता चढ़ि मुल्ला बाग दे, क्या बहिरा हुआ खुदाय॥ (8)

मुल्ला चढ़ि किलकारिया, अलख न बहरा होय।
जिस कारण तू बंग दे, सो दिल ही अन्दर जोय॥ (9)

The world is like a cell of soot
Of which deeds form the doors of ink,
Stones are sown on the earth's surface
And which by pundits has been ruined. (2)

Why dost thou worship lifeless stone
Which throughout life doth answer not?
Blind's that man who cherishes hope
Since he loses honour for nought. (3)

Pilgrimage is the venom tree
Which's spread over age to age;
Kabir has uprooted the tree,
Why should a man this hemlock take? (4)

Men of the world go to temples,
In front of god's idol prostrate;
God dwells in within their own hearts,
So thou must on Him concentrate. (5)

If God's realized by stone worship
Then let me worship a mountain;
Better is the handmill of stone
Since the world feeds on its ground grain. (6)

Stone-made is this human body,
Stone-made is the idol of god,
The worshipper himself is stone-blind,
So worship is not in God's accord. (7)

By assembling gravels and stones
The mosque has been built; on its top
The Mullah shouts cock-a-doodle-do-
Has God hearing perception lost? (8)

The Mullah atop shouts aloud,
The invisible is not deaf;
For what, says Kabir, dost thou muezzin?
God's present within thy own self. (9)

19. भेष कौ अंग

कबीर माला काठ की, कहि समझावै तोहि।
मन न फिरावै आपणों, कहा फिरावै मोहि॥ (1)

माला पहरया कुछ नहीं, गाँठ हिरदा की खोइ।
हरि चरनूँ चित्त राखिये, तो अमरापुर होइ॥ (2)

माला पहरया कुछ नहीं, भगति न आई साथि।
माथों मूँछ मुड़ाइ करि, चल्या जगत के साथि॥ (3)

साँई सेती साँच चलि, औराँ सूँ सुध भाइ।
भावै लम्बे केस करि, भावै घुरड़ि मुड़ाइ॥ (4)

केसों कहा बिगाड़िया, जू मूड़े सौ बार।
मन को काहे न मूड़िए, जामें विषै विकार॥ (5)

तन को जोगी सब करै, मन को बिरला कोइ।
सब सिधि[1] सहजै पाइए, जे मन जोगी होइ॥ (6)

माला पहरया कुछ नहीं, रूल्य मूवा इहि भारि।
बाहरि ढोल्या हींगलू, भीतरि भरी भँगारि॥ (7)

मूड मुडाये हरि मिलै, सब कोई लेहु मुड़ाँय।
बार-बार के मूँडने, भेड़ बैकुठ न जाय॥ (8)

19. Of (Simulative) Guise

The woodmade rosary exhorts
For thee to imbibe, says Kabir,
'Thou dost not turn thy heart away
From desires, so why tell thy beads?' (1)

Wearing the wreath does not avail,
Let the knot of thy heart be freed;
On God's feet concentrate thy mind,
Land of Immortals is achieved. (2)

Wearing the wreath does not avail
If devotion doesn't follow pace;
With thy head and moustache cleanshaved
Thou too dost tread the worldly ways. (3)

With God be sincere and truthful,
And with others be pure and straight;
Then, if thou likest, keep long hair,
Or, with razor thy head cleanshave. (4)

By cleanshaving a hundred times
Thy head why shouldst thou spoil thy hair?
Why dost thou not cleanshave thy heart:
Which doth store many a desire? (5)

All are outwardly ascetic
But deep in heart rare one there is;
Find easy all accomplishments
If the heart has become ascetic. (6)

Wearing the wreath does not avail,
Thou art crushed dead under its weight.
Outside thee dangles the red robe,
Inside thee is full of garbage. (7)

If God is realized by head sheared
All can have their heads cleanshaven,
The sheep sheared again and again
Does not ever go to heaven. (8)

बाना पहरै सिंह का, चलै भेड़ की लार।
बोली-बोले श्याल की, कुत्ता खाये फार॥ (9)

माला फेरत युग गया, पाया न मनका फेर।
करका मनका छाँड़िकै, मनका मनिका फेर॥ (10)

जगत जहंदम राचिया, झूठे कुल की लाज।
तन बिनसे कुल बिनसिहै, गह्वा न राम जिहाज॥ (11)

20. कुसंगति कौ अंग

निरमल बूँद अकास की, पड़ि गई भोमि विकार।
मूल बिनंठा माँनवी, बिन संगति भठछार॥ (1)

मूरिष संग न कीजिए, लोहा जलि न तिराइ।
कदली सीप भवंग मुख, एक बूँद तिहुँ भाइ॥ (2)

मारी मरै कुसंग की, केला काठै बेर।
वो हालै वो चीरिये, साषित[1] संग नबंरि[2]॥ (3)

माखी गुड़ में गड़ि रही, पंष रहीं लपटाइ।
ताली पीटै सिरि धुनैं, मीठें बांई माइ॥ (4)

ऊँचे कुल क्या जनमियाँ, जे करणी ऊँच न होइ।
सोबन कलस सुरे भरया, साधू निंद्या सोइ॥ (5)

Wearing the garb of a tiger
(The hypocrite) paces like sheep,
He doth speak the tongue of the fox
The dog tears him apart and eats. (9)

Telling rosebeads ages have passed
But didn't get straight the twists of heart;
Put the rosary off thy hands,
Tell beads of thy heart in thy heart (10)

The world is created hell, for him
Who's for false honour of household,
With body's end the household ends
If he does not the Ram-ship hold. (11)

20. Of Bad Company

Pure drop of water from the sky
Falls in vain on the earth's surface;
Rootless man in ill-company
Is ashes from a kiln's furnace. (1)

Don't befriend one who is a fool,
Iron does not in waters float;
In banana, oyster, snake mouths
Three way effect has single drop.[1] (2)

The victim of ill-company's
Like banana when briar's beside,
The former sways the latter pricks,
Like a *shaakt*[2] with his new-wed wife. (3)

The fly is glued to jaggery
Wherein all its wings are soaked,
Clap thy hands and beat thy forehead,
Alas! in the sweet it gets choked. (4)

If deeds aren't high, it matters not
If one is born in high household,
A righteous man condemns wholesole
A liquor filled pot made of gold. (5)

21. संगति कौ अंग

कबिरा संगति साधु¹ की, हरै और की व्याधि।
संगति बुरी कुसाधु² की, आठौं पहर उपाधि॥ (1)

काजल केरी कोठड़ी, तैसा यहु संसार।
बलिहारी ता दास की, पैसि रे निकसणहार॥ (2)

कबीर मन पंषी भया, जहाँ मन तहाँ उड़ि जाइ।
जो जैसी संगति करै, सौ तैसे फल खाइ॥ (3)

22. असाध¹ कौ अंग

कबीर भेष अतीत² का, करतूति करैं अपराध।
बाहरि दीसै साध गति, माँहै महा असाध¹॥ (1)

उज्जल देखि न धीजिये, बग ज्यूँ माडै ध्यान॥
धीरे बैठि चपेटसी, यूँ ले बूड़ैं ग्यान॥ (2)

जेता मीठा बोलणाँ, तेता साध न जाँणि।
पहली थाह दिखाइकरि, ऊँडै देसी आँड़ि॥ (3)

वाँबी कूटै बावरे, सर्प न मारा जाय।
मूरख वाँबी नाँ डसै, सरप जगत को खाय॥ (4)

21. Of Company

The company of the righteous
Others sorrows doth mitigate,
While company of the unrighteous
Is grief for all the triad hours eight. (1)

The world is much similar to
A cell where there's soot all around,
That devotee deserves the praise
A spotless escape who has found. (2)

This body has become a bird,
Where it likes it flies, says Kabir,
Man eats the fruit of whatever
Kind of company he doth keep. (3)

22. Of the Unrighteous

Garbed as ascetic, Kabir says,
But in actions of crime involved,
Whose outward seems all righteousness
But inside he is a big fraud. (1)

Don't trust him who's fulgent and neat.
And who seems in wisdom immersed;
Like the crane that seems meditate
But pounces on fish quietly perched. (2)

The sweeter a man speaks, the more
Righteous man thou shouldst not him treat,
Since he first shows shallow waters
But later leads to sink in deep. (3)

Incapable of killing snake
The unrighteous beats the snake-hole;
O thou fool! snake-hole does not sting
But the snake eats the world wholesole. (4)

23. साध¹ कौ अंग

साधू ऐसा चाहिये, दुखै दुखावै नाँहिं।
पान फूल छेरे नहीं, बसै बगीचा माँहि॥ (1)

साधू भौंरा जग कली, निस दिन फिरै उदास।
दुक इक तहाँ बिलंबिया, जहाँ शीतल शब्द निवास॥ (2)

कमल पत्र है साधु जन, बसै जगत के माँहि।
बालक केरी धाय ज्यों, अपना जानत नाहिं॥ (3)

सब बन तो चंदन नहीं, शूरा के दल नाँहिं।
सब समुद्र मोती नहीं, यों साधू जग माहिं॥ (4)

सिंहन के लेहँड़ा नहीं, हंसन की नहिं पाँति।
लालन की ओबरी नहीं, साधु न चले जमाँति॥ (5)

साधू सोई जानिये, चले साधु की चाल।
परमारथ राता रहे, बोले बचन रसाल॥ (6)

बहता पानी निर्मला, बंधा गाँधीला होय।
साधू जन रमते भले, दाग न लागैं कोय॥ (7)

23. Of the Righteous

Such a righteous man we're in need
Who doesn't cause others pain and grief;
Though he lives in a garden but
Doesn't trifle with flowers and leaves. (1)

The righteous-bee in the world-bud
Pensively sad roams day and night,
For a shortwhile he sojourns there
Where cool soothing words are in sight. (2)

Lotus leaves are the righteous men
In the midst of the world who home;
Alike a child's foster-mother
Who doesn't know the child as her own. (3)

All woods are not of sandalwood,
There aren't troops of the chivalrous,
All the seas do not contain pearls,
So in the world are the righteous. (4)

We don't come across lions in hordes,
Swans do not line up in long queues,
There are no bagfuls of diamonds,
So righteous men don't in crowds move. (5)

Know, he only is the righteous
Who steps forward on righteous ways,
With acts of welfare who's in love
And who utters words of sweet taste. (6)

Pure is the water that doth flow,
Noisome puddle is that's stagnant;
So as not to have blots, good are
The righteous who are itinerant. (7)

24. साध साक्षीभूत¹ कौ अंग

संत न छाड़ै संतई, जे कोटिक मिलैं असंत।
चंदन भुवंगा बैठिया, तउ सीतलता न तजंत॥ (1)

कबीर हरि का भाँवता, दूरै थैं दीसंत।
तन षीणा मन उनमना, जग रूठड़ा फिरंत॥ (2)

कबीर हरि का भाँवता, झीणाँ पंजर तास।
रैणि न आवै नींदड़ी, अंगि न चढ़ई मास॥ (3)

जिन्य कुछ जाण्याँ नहीं तिन्ह, सुख नींदड़ी बिहाइ।
मैर अबूझी बूझिया, पूरी पड़ी बलाइ॥ (4)

जिहि घटि जाँण बिनाँण है, तिहि घटि आबंटणाँ घणाँ।
बिन षडै संग्राम है, नित उठि भन सौ झुझुणाँ॥ (5)

फाटै दीदै मैं फिरी, नजरि न आवै कोइ।
जिहि घटि मेरा साईंया, सो क्यूँ छाना होइ॥ (6)

25. साध महिमां¹ कौ अंग

चंदन की कुटकी भली, नाँ बंबुर को अबराऊँ।
बैसनो² की छपरी भलो, ना साषत³ का बड़ गाउँ॥ (1)

24. Of the Righteous in Transcendental State

Saints don't give up their saintliness
Though crores of unsaintly they meet;
Sandalwood doesn't its coolness quit
Though snakes emboss the sandal trees. (1)

One who's dear to God, Kabir says,
Is from a long distance discerned,
He is gaunt but his heart transcends
As if he's quarrelled with the world. (2)

One who is dear to God, Kabir says,
Has slender his bodily frame
At night he lacks sleep and no flesh
His body doth accumulate. (3)

Those who are grossly ignorant,
They have the pleasant carefree sleep,
When I knew this till then unknown
I'd fallen in calamities. (4)

There is intense commotion in
The man's mind who has science and knowledge;
Without sword he fights a battle,
Awake each morn he struggles with himself. (5)

With eyes wide open I wandered
But no one came across my sight;
In whoev'r's heart my Master dwells
How can He remain recondite? (6)

25. Of Magnitude of Righteousness

Wholesome's a piece of sandalwood
Not a wood of acacia trees.
A *vaishnav*'s[1] thatched hut is wholesome,
And not a *shaakt*'s large feudal fief. (1)

जिहँ घर साध न पूजिये, हरि की सेवा नाँहि।
ते घट मुड़हट॑ सारषे, भूत बसै तिन माँहि॥ (2)

क्यूँ नृप नारी नींदयें, क्यूँ पनिहारी॑ कौ मान।
व माँग सँवारे पीव कौं, वा नित उठि सुमिरै राम॥ (3)

कबीर धनि ते सुन्दरी, जिन जाया वैसनो पूत।
राम सुमरि निरभै हुवा, सब जग गया अऊत॑॥ (4)

कबीर भया है केतकी, भँवर भये सब दास।
जहाँ जहाँ भगति कबीर की, तहाँ तहाँ राम निवास॥ (5)

साधू भूँखा भाव का, धन का भूँखा नाँहि।
धन का भूँखा जो फिरैं, सो तो साधू नाँहि॥ (6)

26. सारग्रही कौ अंग

साधू ऐसा चाहिये, जैसा सूप सुभाय।
सार सार को गहि रहै, थोथा देइ बहाय॥ (1)

27. असारग्रही कौ अंग

पापी पुण्य न भाबई, पापहिं बहुत सुहाय।
माखी सुगंध परहरै, जहाँ दुंगधि तहाँ जाय॥ (1)

Home where the righteous isn't welcome,
Nor is there adoration of God,
Such a home is like cremation-site
Whereat spectres and ghosts lodge. (2)

Why is the king's consort condemned,
And why waterwoman's regard?
The former bedecks for her husband,
Each morn the latter adores Ram. (3)

Blest is that woman, says Kabir,
Who gives birth to a *vaishnav* son;
Free from fears she adores Ram,
Know worldwide childless is each one. (4)

Kabir has become a screwpine,
All his devotees became bees,
Therein lies the abode of Ram
Wherever worship is Kabir's[2]. (5)

Righteous man is hungry of feeling,
Hungry of riches he is not;
Hungry of riches one who roams,
Righteous man at all he is not. (6)

26. Of One Who Takes the Substance

Such a righteous man we're in need
Who's like a winnowing basket,
Which doth retain the substance, and,
To blow in wind the chaff doth let. (1)

27. Of One Who Takes the Insubstantial

The sinner does not like goodness
Because on him sin casts a spell;
The fly abandons what's fragrant
But goes where there is stinking smell. (1)

28. उपदेश कौ अंग

ऐसी बानी बोलिये, मन का आपा खोइ।
अपना तन सीतल करै, औरन कौं सुख होइ॥ (1)

जो ताको काँटा बुवै, ताको बो तू फूल।
तोहि फूल के फूल हैं, बाको है तिरसूल॥ (2)

दुर्बल को न सताइये, जाकी मोटी हाय।
बिना जीव की साँस सों, लौह भस्म ह्वै जाय॥ (3)

हाड़ बड़ा हरि भजन करि, द्रव्य बड़ा कछु देह।
अकल बड़ी उपकार कर, जीवन का फल येह॥ (4)

धर्म किये धन ना घटे, नदी न घट्टे नीर।
अपनी आँखे पंखिये, यों कथि कहै कबीर॥ (5)

जग में बैरी कोई नहीं, जो मन सीतल होय।
या आपा को डारि दे, दया करै सब कोय॥ (6)

आवत गारी एक है, उलटत होय अनेक।
कहै कबीर नहिं उलटिये, वाही एक की एक॥ (7)

28. Of Exhortations

Speak in such a soothing manner
That vainglory gets melt away,
Thy own body is calm and cool
And others be joyful and gay. (1)

One who sows prickly thorns for thee
Sow for him flowers that blossom;
For thine flowers thou hast flowers,
His thorns beget tridents for him. (2)

Don't persecute one who is weak
Whose cry of sigh is thick with curses,
A lifeless hide[1] blowing the fire
Doth burn the iron into ashes. (3)

If thy bones are big, adore God,
Give some, if money is immense;
If thy mind's sharp, act for welfare;
This alone is life's fruitful sense. (4)

Religious acts decrease not riches,
Waters of rivers don't abate,
See with thine own eyes (and confirm):
Such a statement Kabir doth make. (5)

Nobody is foe in the world
If thy temper is calm and cool,
Give up thy egotistic pride,
Merciful will be all people. (6)

Single is slander when it comes,
If rejoined many it becomes;
Rejoin it not, exhorts Kabir,
Since his one remains only one. (7)

29. विश्वास कौ अंग

साँई इतना दीजिये, जितना कुटुंब समाय।
ता में भूखा ना रहूँ, साधु न भूखा जाय॥ (1)

भूखा भूखा क्या करै, कहाँ सुनावै लोग।
भाँडा घड़ि जिनि मुख दिया, सोई पूरण जोग॥ (2)

माँगण मरन समान है, बिरला बंचै कोइ।
कहै कबीर रघुनाथ सूँ, मतिर मँगावै मोहि॥ (3)

कबीर तूँ काहै डरै, सिर परि हरि का हाथ।
हस्ती चढ़ि नहिं डोलिये, कूकर भूसैं जु लाख॥ (4)

30. पीव पिछावन कौ अंग

जाके मुँह माथा नहीं, नहीं रूप कुरूप।
पुहुप बास ते पातला, ऐता तत्त अनूप॥ (1)

31. बिर्कताई कौ अंग

मेरे मन में पड़ि गई, ऐसी एक दरार।
फटा फटक पषाँण ज्यूँ, मिलाया न दूजी बार॥ (1)

29. Of Faith

O my Master, give me that much
For my family which's enow;
I mayn't have to live in hunger,
Nor should the righteous hungry go. (1)

Why dost thou shout 'I am hungry',
And let people listen thee shout?
One who has forged this (body) pot,
The same (God) will feed through the mouth. (2)

To beg and to die are equal
From which rarely few can escape;
Even from (bounteous) Raghunath[1]
I mayn't have to beg, Kabir says. (3)

Why shouldst thou fear, affirms Kabir,
Thy head has God's protective arc,
Riding an elephant don't be
Startled though lakhs of dogs may bark. (4)

30. Of Identifying the Lover (God)

God has neither mouth nor forehead,
Handsome or ugly He is not,
He's thinner than flower's fragrance,
Thus, of unique essence He's wrought. (1)

31. Of Reclusion

My heart has cracked such a fissure
Which has no love lost in between,
Alike a rock of quartz once split
Reunited cannot be seen. (1)

कबीर सब जग हंडिया, मंदिल कंधि चढ़ाय¹।
हरि बिन अपना को नहीं, देखे ठोकि बजाय॥ (2)

बड़ा बड़ाई ना तजै, छोटा बहुत इतराय।
ज्यों प्याँदा फरजी भया, टेढ़ा टेढ़ा जाय॥ (3)

32. सम्रथाई कौ अंग

सात समँद की मसि करौ, लेखनि सब बनराइ।
धरती सब कागद करौं, तऊ हरि गुण लिख्या न जाइ॥ (1)

जदि का माई जनमियाँ, कहूँ न पाया सुख।
डाली डाली मैं फिरौं, पातौं पातौं दुख॥ (2)

साँई¹ सों सब होत है, बंदे थे कछु नाँहिं।
राई थैं परबत करे, परबत राई माँहि॥ (3)

हाथी अटक्यों कीच में, काढ़ै को समरत्थ।
की बल निकलै आपने, कि साँई पसारे हत्थ॥ (4)

बुरा जो देखन मैं चला, बुरा न मिलिया कोय।
जो दिल खोजों आपना, तो मुझसा बुरा न कोय॥ (5)

कबिरा सब ते हम बुरे, हमते भला सब कोय।
जिन ऐसा कर बूझिया, मित्र हमारा सोय॥ (6)

The whole world did I discover,
Kabir says, for a permanent home,
Having examined well I found:
Except God no one was my own. (2)

The great does not his greatness quit,
The low too much of air doth take,
When soldier is raised to sergeant
He tends to walk in crooked ways. (3)

32. Of Potence

Let me make paper the whole earth,
And all the forest trees my pen,
Let me make ink of seven seas[1]
But Hari's glory I can't pen. (1)

Since the day mother gave me birth
I did not get happiness ever,
From leaf to leaf I saw sorrow
When branch to branch I did wander. (2)

The Master can do each and all,
While the slave nothing can attain,
(God) can make mountain of mustard,
And a mustard of a mountain. (3)

The elephant's entangled in marsh,
Who's potent him to extricate?
Either he comes out with own strength,
Or to the Master supplicate. (4)

I set out in search of the bad,
No one who was bad did I see,
As much as I do introspect—
There is no one so bad like me. (5)

Among all I'm the worst, says Kabir,
Better than I am is each one;
He who comprehends this truth well,
My friend indeed is the same one. (6)

33. कुशब्द कौ अंग

खूदन तौ धरती सहै, बाढ़ सहै बनराइ।
कुसबद तौ हरिजन सहै, दूजै सह्या न जाय॥ (1)

बोली तो अनमोल है, जो कोई जानै बोलि।
हिये तराजू तौलिये, तब मुख बाहर खोलि॥ (2)

34. सबद[1] कौ अंग

शब्द बराबर धन नहीं, जो कोइ जानै बोलि।
हीरा तो दामों मिले, शब्दहिं मोल न तोल॥ (1)

शब्द बिना सुरति[2] आँधरी, ना जानूँ कित जाय।
द्वार न पाये शब्द का, फिरि फिरि झटका खाय॥ (2)

एक शब्द सुख खानि है, एक शब्द दुख रासि।
एक शब्द बन्धन कटै, एक शब्द गलि फाँसि॥ (3)

35. जीवन मृतक[1] कौ अंग

दीन गरीबी दीन कौ, दुंदर को अभिमान।
दुंदर दिल विष सूँ भरी, दीन गरीबी राम॥ (1)

33. Of the Foul Word

The earth bears the blows of digging,
The forests bear the sweep of floods,
God's men alone bear the foul word,
Which to bear is in no one's guts. (1)

Invaluable is the utterance
For one who knows well the speechways,
For utterance open thy mouth
When thou hast scaled words in heart's scale. (2)

34. Of the Word

Riches aren't equal to the Word,
For one who knows well the speechways,
Diamonds can be had for a price
But the Word's beyond price and weight. (1)

Scriptures are blind without the Word,
Where they lead to, nobody knows,
One who doesn't find door to the Word,
Again and again doth meet shocks. (2)

There is word that's a mine of joy,
There's word that's a heap of sorrows,
There is word that frees from bondage,
There is word that traps neck in noose. (3)

35. Of Life-in-Death

The disputant is with pride fraught
So venom is filled in his heart;
The modest is given poverty,
So he has God as his reward. (1)

कबीर चेरा संत का, दासनि का परदास।
कबीर ऐसे है रहया, ज्यों पाऊँ तलि घास॥ (2)

रोड़ा हैरहो बाट का, तजि पाषंड अभिमान।
ऐसा जे जन है रहै, ताहि मिलै भगवान॥ (3)

कबीर काया समुद्र है, अंत न पावै कोय।
मृतक होय के जो रहै, मानिक लावै सोय॥ (4)

तन समुद्र मन मर्जिवा², एक बार धसि लेय।
की तो लाल ले नीकसे, कि लालच जिय देय॥ (5)

36. चित कपटी कौ अंग

हेत प्रीति सौं जो मिलै, ताको मिलिये धाय।
अंतर राखै जो मिले तासो मिलै बलाय॥ (1)

37. गुरूसिष हेरा¹ कौ अंग

ऐसा कोई ना मिला, समुझै सैन² सुजान।
ढोल बाजता ना सुनै, सुरति³ बिहूना कान॥ (1)

जिन ढूँढया तिन पाइयाँ, गहरे पानी पैठि।
मैं बैरा बूड़न डरा, रहा किनारे बैठि॥ (2)

Kabir[1] is the disciple of saints—
Meek devotee of devotees,
So Kabir lives in such a way
As under the feet grass is meek. (2)

Giving up hypocrisy and pride
Who's (like) a pebble on the road,
In such a way which men can live,
They are the men who realize God. (3)

This body's the sea, Kabir says,
None can see its infinity,
One who doth live a life-in-death
He alone doth bring the ruby. (4)

If the heart-diver for one time
Into the body-sea doth dive,
Either he comes out with rubies,
Or, in greed doth part with his life. (5)

36. Of the Perfidious

One who meets thee with warmth of love
Thou must meet running fast to him;
Who meets thee in perfidy,
Know he himself has met a fiend. (1)

37. Of Guru-Disciple Search

It's rare to come across a man
With symbols able to conceive,
When the ear is without perception
Drum beat too one may not perceive. (1)

Those who embarked on search, they got,
Into deep waters they did dive,
I, the slow-witted, feared to drown
So kept on sitting at sea-side. (2)

38. हेत प्रीति स्नेह कौ अंग

कमोदनी जल हरि बसै, चंदा बसे अकासि।
जो जाही का भाँवता, सो वाही के पास॥ (1)

39. सूरा तन कौ अंग

कबीर मेरे संसा को नहीं, हरि सू लागा हेत।
काम क्रोध सूँ झूझणाँ, चौड़ि माड्या खेत॥ (1)

जिस मरने थे जग डरै, सो मेरे आनंद[1]।
कब मरिहूँ कब देखिहूँ, पूरन परमानंद॥ (2)

कायर बहुत पमाँवही, बहकि न बोले सूर।
काँम पड़्या ही जाँणिहै, किसके मुख परि नूर॥ (3)

कबीर यह घरि प्रेम का, खाला[2] का घर नाँहि।
सीस उतारे हाथ करि[3], सो पैसे घर माँहि॥ (4)

प्रेम न खेतों नीपजै, प्रेम न हाट बिकाइ।
राजा प्रजा जिस रूचै, सिर दे सो ले जाइ॥ (5)

कबीर घोड़ा प्रेम का, चेतनि चढ़ि असवार।
ग्यान षड्ग महिकाल सिरि, भली मचाई मार॥ (6)

38. Of Love and Affection

The water-lily dwells in water,
Whereas the moon dwells in the sky,
Whoever's enamoured of whom
The same one close by him doth lie. (1)

39. Of Bravery

I'm free from doubts, says Kabir,
As I am deep in love with God,
I've to fight against lust and wrath
In a field that is wide and broad. (1)

Death which holds the world in terror
Is a matter of joy for me
The sooner I die the sooner
I see god-of-joy in entirety. (2)

The coward boasts of very much,
Never talks irrelevant the brave,
Know that the task is carried out
By him brightness shines on whose face. (3)

This home is of love, says Kabir,
And not the lodge where aunt[1] dwells in,
The brave, who himself makes shorter
By the head, can then there home in. (4)

Love does not shoot forth in the field,
Love isn't for sale in the market,
Whether king or subject, whoever
Likes, may take bowing down his head. (5)

On the horse of love, says Kabir,
Awakened Mind, the rider, rode,
And with his sword of wisdom hit
Time's head and a pitched battle fought. (6)

जेते तारे रैंणि के, तेते बैरी मुझ।
धड़ सूली सिर कंगुरैं⁴, तऊ न बिसारौं तुझ॥ (7)

40. काल¹ कौ अंग

झूठे सुख को सुख कहैं, मानत है मन मोद।
खलक² चबीणाँ³ काल का, कुछ मुख में कुछ गोद॥ (1)

आजक, काल्हिक निस हमें, मारगि माल्हंता।
काल सिचाणाँ नर चिड़ा, औझड़ आच्यंताँ॥ (2)

सब जग सोता नींद भरि, संत न आवैं नींद।
काल खड़ा सिर ऊपरै, ज्यूँ तोरण आया बींद⁴॥ (3)

आज कहै हरि काल्हि भाजौंगा, काल्हि कहे फिरि काल्हि।
आज ही काल्हि करंतडाँ, औसर जैसी चालि॥ (4)

कबीर पल की सुधि नहीं, करै काल्हि का साज।
काल अच्यंता झड़पसी, ज्यूँ तीतर को बाज॥ (5)

मैं अकेला ए दोइ जणाँ, छेती नाँहि काँइ।
जे जम आगै ऊबरौं, तो जुरा पहूँती आइ॥ (6)

जो उग्या सो आथवे, फूल्या सो कुमिलाइ।
जो चिणियाँ सो ढहि पड़ें, जो आया सो जाइ॥ (7)

As many are stars of the night
So many are 'nemies of me;
Let my trunk on gibbet and head
On turret fall, I mayn't forg't thee. (7)

40. Of Time/ Death

One who treats false pleasure as real,
And gets ecstatic in his views,
He knows not man is food of Time[1]
Who holds some in lap, some in jaws. (1)

Today, tomorrow, in the night,
On the pathway, all of a sudd'n,
Very soon, not far off in time,
The Time-hawk will kill the man-bird. (2)

The whole world is lost in sopor,
But insomniac becomes the saint,
Death doth stand just over the head
As bridegroom under welcome-gate. (3)

'I shall adore God tomorrow',
Next day too 'tomorrow' he says;
Thus by repeated postponement
Tomorrows become yesterdays. (4)

Man's ignorant of the moment
But for tomorrow doth equip;
Unawares Time doth lay the seize
Much like the hawk doth the partridge. (5)

I'm alone and they are two,
Between the two there's no difference,
If somehow there's escape from Death,
Senility has arrivance (6)

What rises (in the sky) doth set down,
What blossoms that doth fade away,
What's erected that doth collapse,
What comes that has to go away. (7)

जो पहरया सो फाटिसी, नाँव धरया सो जाइ।
कबीर सोई तत्त गहि, जो गुरू दिया बताइ॥ (8)

कबीर यहु जग कुछ नहीं, बिन षारा षिन मीठ।
कालि्ह जो बैठा माड़िया, आज नसाँणा दीठ॥ (9)

निधड़क बैठा राम बिनु, चेतनि करै पुकार।
यहु तन जल का बुलबुला, विनसत नाहीं बार॥ (10)

पाँणी केरा बुदबुदा, इसी हमारी जाति।
एक दिनाँ छिप जाँहिगें, तारे ज्यूँ परभाति॥ (11)

पंथी ऊभा पंथ सिरि, बुगचा बान्ध्या पूठि।
मरणाँ मुँह आगै खड़ा, जीवन का सब झूठ॥ (12)

विष के वन में घर किया, सरप रहे लपटाइ।
ताथै जियरे डरै गह्या, जागत रैणि बिहाइ॥ (13)

कबीर सब सुख राम है और दुखाँ की रासि।
सुर नर मुनिवर असुर सब पड़े काल की पासि॥ (14)

जिनि हम जाए ते मुए, हम भी चालणहार।
जे हमको आगे मिले, तिन भी बंध्या मार॥ (15)

कान्हि करै सो आज कर, सब साँज तेरे साथ।
कालि्ह, कालि्ह तू क्या करैं, कान्हि काल के हाथ॥ (16)

Whatever is worn that gets torn,
Whatever name's assumed that ends;
So of guru's exhortations
Kabir doth hold the quintessence. (8)

Nought is this world, opines Kabir,
This moment salty, sweet the next,
Behold! to ruin has come today
What yesterday did stand bedecked. (9)

Without Ram thou dost sit carefree!
Be awake! remember His name;
This body's a water bubble
And takes not much of time to fade. (10)

The way bubbles rise in water,
Similar is our (human) race,
In a day it will evanesce
As in early morning stars fade. (11)

With pack of load tied on his back
The traveller at road end stood,
There he was face to face with Death,
Since in human life all's falsehood. (12)

I homed in forest of venom
Where snakes entwined all around trees,
With that my heart lay gripped in fear,
So I passed the night without sleep. (13)

Ram's all happiness, says Kabir,
The rest is a heap of sorrows,
Gods, humans, saints and devils, all
Easily fall within Time's noose. (14)

They departed who preced'd us,
We too are in the goers' train,
All those who will meet us ahead,
Mortal they also will remain. (15)

Do today what thou wilt tomorrow,
As thou hast all the equipment,
Why dost thou harp on tomorrow?
Since tomorrow is in Time's hand. (16)

कालिह करे सो आज कर, आज करे सो अब्ब।
पल में परलै होइगी, बहुरि करेगा कब्ब॥ (17)

घरी जु बाजै राजदर, सुनता है सब कोइ।
आयु घटे जोबन खिसै, कुशल कहाँ ते होइ॥ (18)

तरूवर पात सौं यौ कहे, सुनो पात एक बात।
यह घर याही रीति है, इन आवत इक जात॥ (19)

मछली दह छूटै नहीं, झीवर मेरा काल।
जेहि जेहि डावर घर करों, तहँ तहँ मेले जाल॥ (20)

खुलि खेलो संसार में, बाँधि न सक्कै कोय।
घाट जगाति॰ क्या करें, सिर पर पोट न होय॥ (21)

चलती चाकी देखिकै, दिया कबीरा रोय।
दो पाटन बिच आइके साबत गया न कोय॥ (22)

मंदिर माँहि झबूकती, दीवा कैसी जोति।
हंस बटाऊ चलि गया, काढ़ौ घर की छोति॥ (23)

बारी बारी आवर्णीं, चले पियारे म्यंत।
तेरी बारी रे जिया, नेड़ी आवें चिंत॥ (24)

Do today what thou wilt tomorrow,
Do just now what thou wilt today,
When wilt thou do many a lot?
In a moment Deluge will sway. (17)

At the king's court, everybody
Doth listen to the clock's chiming[2],
Age doth decrease and youth doth budge,
How can there be any well-being? (18)

The tree doth to the leaf say thus:
'O Leaf', listen to what I say:
In this house there's the tradition—
One comes, the other goes away'. (19)

The fish does not leave the water-pond,
It says, 'The fisher is my death,
Whatever lake I make my home,
In the same lake he spreads his net'. (20)

Play free and open in this world,
Since nobody can keep thee bound,
At Toll-bridge helpless is the Taxer
When on thy head no load is found. (21)

Watching the running water-mill
Kabir became sad and he wept,
Having come between two mill-blocks
Not a single is left intact. (22)

Similar to light of a lamp
Soul illumines the body-house,
When swan-sojourner doth depart
The untouchable's[3] taken out. (23)

Turn by turn and in their own turns
So many dear friends passed away,
Now o human! it is thy turn
Which is fast approaching each day. (24)

41. संजीवनी[1] कौ अंग

जहाँ जुरा मरण व्यापै नहीं, मुवा न सुणिये कोइ।
चलि कबीर तिहि देसड़े, जहाँ वैद विधाता होइ॥ (1)

कबीर हरि चरणौं चल्या, माया मोह थे टूटि।
गगन मंडल आषण किया, काल गया सिर कूटि॥ (2)

तरवर तास बिलांबिए, बारह मास फलंत।
सीतल छाया गहर फल, पंषी केलि करंत॥ (3)

जाको राखै साँइया, मार न सकिहै कोय।
बाल न बंका करि सकै, जो जग बैरी होय॥ (4)

42. अपारिख कौ अंग

पाइ पदारथ पेलि करि, कंकर लीया हाथि।
जोड़ी बिछुटी हंस की, पड़्या बँगा के साथि॥ (1)

एक अचंभा देखिया, हीरा हाटि बिकाइ।
परिषणहारे बाहिरा, कौड़ी बदले जाइ॥ (2)

कबीर गुदड़ी बीषरी, सौदा गया बिकाइ।
खोटा बाँध्या गाँठड़ी, इथ कुछ लिया न जाइ॥ (3)

41. Of Elixir

Where old age and death don't prevail,
Where none do hear of someone's death,
Let's go to that land, says Kabir,
Where the Healer-Creator doth dwell. (1)

Freed from attachment and maya
At God's feet Kabir did prostrate,
In the skyey clime made his seat,
Seeing this Time did lament make. (2)

Sojourn and rest under the Tree
That bears fruit around the whole year,
There is cool shade and fruits profound,
And over which birds play and twitter. (3)

He whom the Master doth protect
No one ever his death can cause,
Not a minor hurt can him hurt
Though men of the world are his foes. (4)

42. Of the Non-Assayer

Throwing out bounty of nature
One who grabs shingles in his hands;
Thus, swan couple parts from each other
To fall in the company of cranes. (1)

One wonder I chanced to come across—
Diamonds were in the market sold;
Absent were the skilled assayers
So for cowries they were disposed. (2)

This life's bedding stands scattered,
Marketing is done, Kabir says,
The counterfeit has packed his baggage
But nothing from this world can take. (3)

पैडै मोती बिखरया, अंधा निकस्या आइ।
जोति बिना जगदीश की, जगत उलंघ्या जाइ॥ (4)

कबीर यह जगु अंधला, जैसी अंधी गाइ।
बछा था सो मरि गया, ऊभो चाम चटाइ॥ (5)

43. पारिख कौ अंग

जब गुण कूँ गाहक मिलै, तब गुण लाख बिकाइ।
जब गुण को गाहक नहीं, तब कौड़ी बदले जाइ॥ (1)

44. उपजणि¹ कौ अंग

नाँव न जाणै गाँव का, मारगि लागा जाऊँ।
कालि्ह जु काटा भाजिसी, पहिली क्यों न खड़ाऊँ॥ (1)

कबीर सुपिणै हरि मिल्या, सूताँ लिया जगाइ।
आषि न मीचौं डरपता, मति सुपिणाँ है जाइ॥ (2)

गोव्यंदक के गुण बहुत हैं, लिखे जु हिरदै माँहि।
डरता पाँणी ना पिऊँ, मति वे धोये जाँहि॥ (3)

ऊँचा चढ़ि असमान कूँ, मेरू उलंघे ऊड़ि।
पसू पखेरू जीव जंत, सब रहै मेर² में बूड़ि॥ (4)

Along the path pearls are scattered,
Ignorant the blind passes on;
So without inward light of God,
Man through this world goes hopping on. (4)

This world is blind, opines Kabir,
Much similar to that blind cow
Which had a calf but long back dead,
She standing licks the calf-skin now. (5)

43. Of the Assayer

When there are takers of virtues,
Virtues sell for lakhs of rupees,
Where there're no takers of virtues,
They are exchanged for mere cowries. (1)

44. Of Origin of Devotion

I do not know the village's name,
But I have set out on my way;
Tomorrow thorn will pierce my foot,
Why didn't I wear footwear woodmade? (1)

In dream Kabir chanced to meet God,
Who awakened him from his sleep,
Fearful he does not close his eyes
Lest the dream may remain a dream. (2)

Many are the attributes of God,
Which in heart are in black and white,
Fearful I dare not drink water
Lest they get washed by oversight. (3)

Familial ties fly in the sky
And hop across the Meru's[1] peak;
Birds, brutes, beasts and animals are
In familial ties immersed deep. (4)

45. कस्तूरियाँ मृग कौ अंग

कस्तूरी कुंडलि बसै, मृग ढूँढै वन माँहि।
ऐसे घटि घटि राम हैं, दुनियाँ देखे नाँहि॥ (1)

सो साँई तन में बसै, भ्रम्यौ न जाणौं तास।
कस्तूरी के मृग ज्यूँ, फिर फिर सूघैं घास॥ (2)

कबीर खोजी राम का, गया जु सिंघल द्वीप।
राम तो घट भीतर रमि रह्या, जो आवै परतीत॥ (3)

घटि बाँधि कहीं न देखिये, ब्रह्म रह्या भरपूरि।
जिनि जान्याँ तिन निकट है, दूरि कहै थै दूरि॥ (4)

मैं जाण्याँ हरि दूर है, हरि रह्या सकल भरपूरि।
आप पिछाणौं बाहिरा, नेड़ा की थै दूरि॥ (5)

46. निंदा कौ अंग

दोख पराये देखि करि, चल्या हँसत हँसत।
अपने च्यंति न आवई, जिनकी आदि न अंत॥ (1)

निंदक नेड़ा राखिये, आँगणि कुटी बँधाइ।
बिन साबण पानी बिना, निरमल करै सुभाइ॥ (2)

45. Of the Musk Deer

Musk lies in the musk deer's own nave,
But roams in forest it to seek;
Alike, God pervades heart to heart,
But men of the world don't conceive. (1)

In man himself the Master dwells,
But man deluded knows not this,
Much similar to a musk deer
Again and again the grass sniffs. (2)

The seeker of Ram, says Kabir,
To the Singhal Island[1] did march;
When in himself he got convinced,
He found Ram pervade in his heart. (3)

God exists profuse in each place,
So don't think less here and more there,
Those who say 'He's far', He's far,
Those who know Him near, He's near. (4)

I knew God to be far away,
But He is ubique, here and there;
Thou didst know Him to be far off,
He's far off though very near. (5)

46. Of Vituperation

Seeking blemishes in others
Those who laugh and sarcasting tend,
They ignore their own blemishes
Which have no beginning nor end. (1)

Near thee keep a vitup'rator,,
In thy courtyard erect him a hut,
He washes thee sparklingly clean
Without soap and without water. (2)

निन्दक दूर न कीजिए, दीजै आदर माँन।
निरमल तन मन सब करै, बकि बकि आँनहि आन॥ (3)

आपण यौं न सराहिए, और न कहिये रंक।
नाँ जाणौ किस ब्रिष तलि, कूड़ा होइ करंक॥ (4)

कबीर आप ठगाइये और न ठगिये कोइ।
आप ठग्याँ सुख उपजै, और ठग्याँ दुख होइ॥ (5)

अब की जे साँई मिलै, तो सब दुख आपौं रोइ।
चरनूँ ऊपर सीस धरि, कहूँ जु कहणाँ होइ॥ (6)

निन्दक एकहु मति मिलै, पापी मिलौ हजार।
एक निन्दक के सीस पर, हजार पाप को भार॥ (7)

निन्दक ते कुत्ता भला, हठ कर माँडै रारि।
कूकर तै क्रोधी बुरा, गुरू दिवावै गारि॥ (8)

कबिरा मेरे साधु की, निन्दा करौ मत कोइ।
जो पै चन्द कलंक है, तऊ उजियारा होइ॥ (9)

जो कोई निन्दै साधु कों, संकट आवै सोइ।
नरक माँहि जन्मे मरै, मुक्ति न कबहूँ होइ॥ (10)

Don't distance a vitup'rator,
Rather give him respect and honour;
He keeps thy body and heart clean
Exaggerating faults of others. (3)

Don't extol thyself so as to
Nickname others paltry and vain,
Nobody knows under which tree
A bone the garbage may contain. (4)

It is better to be cheated
Than to cheat others, says Kabir,
Being cheated begets happiness,
But cheating others begets grief. (5)

If this time I chance to meet God,
I shall weep and well up my grief,
I shall place my head at His feet
And go forth whatever to plead. (6)

Let none meet a vitup'rator,
Thousand sinners he may come on;
A burden of a thousand sins
One vitup'rator's head bears on. (7)

Better than a vituperator
Is self-willed dog that doth assail,
Worse than the dog is man of wrath,
Who to his guru brings bad name. (8)

Kabir says," "My men of righteousness
Should be vituperated not.
Light is showered all around though
The moon has the blemishing spot". (9)

One who vitup'rates the righteous,
Catastrophe on him doth fall,
He is born in hell and there dies,
Salvation he doesn't get at all. (10)

47. निगुणाँ कौ अंग

झिरमिरि झिरमिरि बरसिया, पाँहण ऊपरि मेह।
माटी गलि सैजल भई, पाँहण बोही तेह॥ (1)

48. विनती कौ अंग

कबीर साँई तो मिल्हगै, पूछिहिंगे कुसलात।
आदि अंति की कहूँगा, उर अंतर की बात॥ (1)

कबीर भूलि बिगाड़िया, तू नाँ करि मैला चित।
साहब गरवा लोड़िये, नफर बिगाड़ै नित॥ (2)

करता करै बहुत गुण, औगुँण कोई नाँहि।
जे दिल खोजो आपणाँ, तौ सब औगुण मुझ माँहि॥ (3)

साहब तुम जनि बीसरौ, लाख लोग मिलि जाँहि।
हमसे तुमकूँ बहुत है, तुमसे हमको नाँहि॥ (4)

49. बेलि[1] कौ अंग

कबिरा कड़ई बेलड़ी, कड़ुवा ही फल होइ।
साध नाँव तब पाइये, जब बेलि बिछोहा होइ॥ (1)

47. Of the Virtueless

It drizzled in graceful drizzles,
On the stone fell showers of rain,
Soil melted when it got watered,
But the stone showed no mark of change. (1)

48. Of Entreaty

When I meet my Master, says Kabir
About my well-being He'll ask,
From the beginning to the end
I'll tell what lies deep in my heart. (1)

Error undid thee, Kabir says,
But thou needst not sadd'n thy mind,
What's desired is solemn Master
Since the servant errs many times. (2)

Many are Creator's attributes,
Blemishes none at all has He;
When I introspect, then, I find
All the blemishes are in me. (3)

O my Saheb! forget me not
Though lakhs of people Thou mightst meet,
Like me thou hast many and many,
Like thee I have none (I entreat). (4)

49. Of the Creeper

Of bitter taste is this (world) creeper,
Its fruit as well bitterly tastes;
The true name of God is attained
When from the creeper man sep'rates. (1)

50. अबिहड़[1] कौ अंग

कबीर साथी सो किया, जाके सुख दुख नहिं कोइ।
हिलि मिलि है करि खेलिस्यूँ, कदै बिछोह न होइ॥ (1)

कबीर सिरजनहार बिन, मेरा हितू न कोइ।
गुण औगुण बिहड़ैं नहीं, स्वारथ बंधी लोइ॥ (2)

अर्ब खर्ब[2] लौं द्रव्य है उदे अस्त लौं राज।
भक्ति महातम न तुलै, ई सब कौने काज॥ (3)

आगि जो लागी समुद्र में, धूआँ प्रगट न होय।
सो जाने जो जरि मुआ, जाकी लाई होय॥ (4)

आगि जो लागी समुद्र महँ जरे जौ काँदो झारि।
पूर्व पछिम के पंडिता मुए विचारि विचारि॥ (5)

आज काल दिन कइक में स्थिर नाँही शरीर।
कैतिक दिन राखिवौं, काचै बासन नीर॥ (6)

आस्ति कहौं तो कोइ न पतीजै बिआस्ति का सिद्धा।
कहहिं कबीर सनहु हे सन्तो हीरी हीरहिं विद्धा॥ (7)

एक एक निरूवारिये, जो निरूवारी जाय।
दुइ मुख को बोलना घना तमाचा खाय॥ (8)

50. Of the Indivisible

Kabir has befriended that One
Who has neither delight nor dole,
Intimate with Him he will play
And from Him not part with at all. (1)

Except the Creator, says Kabir,
There is no well-wisher of mine;
Men fail to distinguish virtue
From vice since they've an axe to grind. (2)

Money in millions and billions
And sunrise to sunset kingdom;
Of what use they are? They weigh not
Equal to the grace of devotion. (3)

Inside the heart there burns the fire
But nowhere's visible the smoke;
He feels the fire who in it burns,
Or, the setter of the fire knows. (4)

Even the wet bottom mud burnt
When the ocean was in fire caught;
The pundits of the north and south
Did die of speculative thought. (5)

Today, tomorrow or within
A few days ends this mortal frame;
For how long can a kutcha pot
Within it the water retain? (6)

To say God is, no one believes,
'There's no God' is hard to propound,
O saints, listen! invokes Kabir,
It's diamond that cuts diamond. (7)

Quit all thy desires one by one
Only then thou canst seek quittance,
An instrument of percussion
Is slapped hard in each of its ends. (8)

एक कहूँ तो है नहीं, दुई कहौं तो गारि।
है जैसा तैसा रहो कहहि कबीर पुकारि॥ (9)

कुरू बहियाँ बल आपनी छाड़ु बिरानी आसु।
जे (घर) अंगना नदिया बहे सो कस मरत पियास॥ (10)

काल खड़ा सिर ऊपरै, जागि बिराने मीत।
जाके घर है गेल में सो कैसे सोवे निचींत॥ (11)

चलते चलते पगु थका नगर रहा नव कोस।
बीचहि में डेरा पड़ा कहो कवन को दोस॥ (12)

चौगोड़ा के देखते व्याधा भागो जाय।
एक अचंभा हो देखा मरा काठ को खाय॥ (13)

जब लगि ढोला तब लगि बोला, तब लगि धन व्यवहार।
ढोला फूट धन गया कोई न झाँकै द्वार॥ (14)

जब लगि तारा जगमगै, तब लगि उगै न सूर।
जब लगि जीव कर्म बस डोले तब लगि ज्ञान न पूर॥ (15)

जरा मरण बालापना चारि अवस्था आइ।
जस मुसवहि तके बिलाइया अस जम घात लगाइ॥ (16)

जहँ गाहक तह हौं नहीं हौं तहँ गाहक नाँहि।
बिनु विवेक भरमत फिरै, देखि शब्द की छाँहि॥ (17)

If I say (God) is one, He's not,
If I say two, it's an abuse,
Let it so remain what it is,
Thus Kabir says in shouts profuse. (9)

Trust on the strength of thy own arms,
Pinned on others give up thy hope;
Why should he ever die of thirst?
Yonder whose house a river flows. (10)

Death doth stand just over thy head,
In alien land, friend, be awake!
One who lives in a narrow street,
A carefree sleep how canst he take? (11)

I walked and walked so my feet tired,
Twice nine miles the town did remain,
In the midway I had to halt,
Far this lapse, say, who is to blame? (12)

No sooner did the poacher see
The quadrup'd than he ran for good,
I happened to witness a wonder—
The dead devouring the firewood. (13)

So long as there's drum there's sound,
And till then money matters sweep,
The drum breaks down, money goes out,
Then into thy door none do peep. (14)

(In the sky) so long as stars twinkle
Till that time the sun does not rise,
So long as man roams bound to deeds
Till that time he is pseudowise. (15)

Childhood, youth, old age and next death—
Four stages are in man's life-span,
Like the cat that watches the rat
So to lay seize Death waits on man. (16)

I am not where there are takers,
Where there are takers I'm not there,
Chasing the shadow of the Word
With lack of wisdom I wander. (17)

जाके सद्गुर नहिं मिला ब्याकुल चहुँ दिसि धाव।
आँखि न सूझै बावरे घर जर घूर बताव॥ (18)

जेते पत्र वनस्पति और गंगा के रेणु।
पंडित बिचारा क्या कहे कबीर कहा मुख वेणु॥ (19)

ज्ञान रत्न की कोठरी, चुपक दिया है ताल।
पारखु आगे खोलिये कुंजी बचन रसाल॥ (20)

ढिग बूड़े उछले नहीं इहै अंदेसा मोहि।
सलिल मोह की धार में का निंदिआई तोहि॥ (21)

तीनि लोक टीढ़ि भया उड़े मन के साथ।
हरि जाने बिनु भटके परे काल के हाथ॥ (22)

तीनि लोक चोरी भया सर्वस सब का लीन्ह।
बिना मूड का चोरवा परा न काहू चीन्ह॥ (23)

तीनि लोक भो पींजरा, पाप पुण्य भो जाल।
सकल जियरा सावज भया एक अहेरी काल॥ (24)

तीरथ गए ते बहि मुए, जूड़े पाणि नहाय।
कहहि कबीर पुकारि के राक्षस होत पछताय॥ (25)

तीरथ गए दू जना चित चंचल मन चोर।
एको पाप न काटिया, मन दस लादै और॥ (26)

Man, who doesn't get a true guru,
Runs restless four directionward;
Blind, he can't see his house in fire
So puts off fire in the wasteyard. (18)

Pundits fail to state so Kabir
Ventures to transmit the message:
That uncountable are desires like
Tree leaves and sand-grains in the Ganges. (19)

The cell of precious-stones-of-wisdom
Is locked with the silence-lock,
Unlock it before the assayer
With the key of honey-sweet talk. (20)

Near the brink thou didst drown, for escape
Thou didst not jump out; I suspect this:
That the tempting water current
Hast made thee fall into a sleep. (21)

All the three worlds became locusts,
With desires flew to skyey clime,
Ignorant of God they did roam
And fell into the hands of Time. (22)

In all the three worlds theft took place,
All belongings of all were taken,
But Maya the thief without head
Was identified by no one. (23)

All the three worlds are like a cage,
Net like are sins and acts of grace,
All the living beings are deers
For Time the mighty hunter's sake. (24)

Cold water bath led them to death
Those for their pilgrimage who went;
So Kabir says in shouts aloud
Reborn as devils they repent. (25)

Wavering-mind and Thievish-Heart—
These two embarked on pilgrimage,
Not a single sin was washed, rather,
With ten mounds of sin homeward came. (26)

दर्पण के गुफामहँ सोनहा पैठे धाय।
देखे प्रतिमा आपनी, भूँकि भूँकि मरि जाय॥ (27)

पाँवहि पहुमी नापते, दरिया करते फाल।
हाथन्हि पर्वत तौलते, तेहि धरि खायो काल॥ (28)

पानी ते अति पातला धूम्र ते अति क्षीण।
पवनहु ते उतावला दोस्त कबीरनि कीन्ह॥ (29)

बेरा बाँधिनि सर्प का, भवसागर अति माह।
छोड़े तो बूड़े नहीं, गहे तो डसे बाँह॥ (30)

बेलि कुढंगी फल निफरो, फुलवा कुबुद्धि गंधाय।
और विनष्टी तुंबिका, सरो पात करूवाय॥ (31)

मन गयन्द मानै नहीं चले सुरति के साथ।
महावत विचारा क्या करें जो अंकुश नहिं हाथ॥ (32)

मनिषा जनम दुलभ है होय न दूजी बार।
पक्का फल जो झरि परै बहुरि न लागै डार॥ (33)

मानुष का गुण ही बड़ा माँस न आवै काज।
हाड़ न होते आभरण त्वचा न बाजन बाज॥ (३४)

हौं तो सब ही की कहीं मेरी कहे न कोय।
मेरी कहे सो जना जो मुझ ही सा होय॥ (35)

Into the cave of bright mirrors
The dog happened to make his race;
In mirrors saw his own image
So barked and died in barking state. (27)

Who[1] with footsteps measured the earth,
Who[2] did the sea split asunder,
Who[3] weighed mountain lifting in hands,
Death seized them and ate soon after. (28)

Kabir has befriended that One
Who's much more fluid than water,
Very much thinner than smoke,
And compared to wind much faster. (29)

In the vast sea of mundanity
Desires are snake ships in car'van,
If one deserts them one drowns not,
If one holds them they sting on arms. (30)

This world is ill-formed creeper with
Fruits sans taste and blooms of foul smell,
Ruinous colocynth it doth bear,
In its leaves bitterness doth swell. (31)

This heart-elephant doesn't obey
And accompanies Mammon's band,
What the helpless mahout may do!
Since he hasn't whiptool in his hand. (32)

It is rare to have human life,
This human body isn't again,
The fruit fallen down from the tree
Does not stick to the branch again. (33)

For his qualities man is great,
Not for his flesh which goes unused,
Nor do his bones make ornaments,
Nor doth his skin to a drum glued. (34)

Of everybody I speak,
But nobody doth speak of me,
Of me only that man can speak
Who's similarity with me. (35)

रतन का जतन करि माटी का सिंगार।
आया कबीरा फिरि गया फीका है संसार॥ (36)

रही एक की भई अनेक की विश्वा बहु भर्तारी।
कहहिं कबीर काके संग जरिहै बहुत पुरुष की नारी॥ (37)

राउर[3] के पिछुवारे गाबैं चारों सैन।
जीव परा बहु लूट मै नहिं कुछ लेन न देन॥ (38)

राह विचारी क्या करे, जो पन्थि न चलै सुधारि।
अपनी मारग छाँड़ि के फिरै उजारि उजारि॥ (39)

लोहा केरी नावरी पाहन गरुहा भार।
सिर पर विष की पोटरी उतरन चाहे पार॥ (40)

शेख तकी मैं बन्दा तेरा झगरा एक निबेरहु मेरा।
प्रगट कहौ कि परदा मुरगी के जो अंडा होते अविरत की है
मरदा॥ (41)

हीरा सोई सराहिये सहे जो घन का चोट।
कपट कुरंगी मानवा परखत निकला खोट॥ (42)

शब्द हमारा तू शब्द का सुनि मति जाहु सरिक्क।
जो चाहहु निज तत्व को शब्दहु लेहि परखि॥ (43)

तन संशय मन सुनहा काल अहेरी नीत।
एक हि डांग बसेउबा कुशल पूछहु काहू मीत॥ (44)

The human cares for precious stones
And embellishes the clay (body).
Kabir came here but soon went back,
The world tastes of insipidity. (36)

(Married) to one but owned by many
This world's a polyandrous woman,
Along with whom will she be burnt
A woman of many a man? (37)

In the backyard of king's palace
Soldiers of four-pronged army sing;
In loot are engrossed all humans
But unconcerned is the king. (38)

Helpless is the path if careful
In walking isn't the wayfarer;
Having diverged from the right path
In wilderness he doth wander. (39)

Thy boat is composed of iron
Which is heavily loaded with stones;
With thy poison-pack on thy back
How canst thou wish to land beyond? (40)

O Sheikh Taki![5] I'll be thy slave,
Settle a dispute for my sake!
Say in unequivocal terms—
If hen's egg is male or female? (41)

Extend thy praise to that diamond
Which can bear a sledgehammer's blows;
Ill-meaning hypocrite is proved
Fake when a test he undergoes. (42)

The Word's ours, thou art of the Word,
So hearing it thou shouldst not steal,
If thou desirest the essence,
Test well the Word, so says Kabir. (43)

O friend! Why enquire my well-being?
Each day Death-hunter is about,
With His stick's single blow to scourge
This heart-dog with body of doubts. (44)

कबीर समुद्र न छोड़िये, जो अति खारो होय।
पोखरि' पोखरि ढूँढते भली न कहियों कोय॥ (45)

कबीरा हमरा कोई नहीं, हम किसहूँ के नाँहि।
जिन यह रचन रचाइया, तित ही माँहि समाँहि॥ (46)

51. निगुरानर कौ अंग

कोटिक चन्दा ऊगवै, सूरज कोटि हजार।
सतगुरू मिलिया बाहिरे, दीसे घोर अँधियार॥ (1)

जो कामिनी परदा रहै, सुने न गुरू मुख बात।
सो तो होगी शूकरी फिरै उघारै गात॥ (2)

52. स्वारथ कौ अंग

सुख के सगै हैं स्वारथी, दुख में रहे जो दूरि।
कहै कबीर परमारथी, दुख सुख सदा हजूरि॥ (1)

53. परमारथ कौ अंग

मरूँ पर माँगू नहीं, अपने तन के काज।
परमारथ के कारने, मोहि न आवै लाज॥ (1)

Don't desert the sea salty though
It is in excess, Kabir says,
Nobody takes it in good light
To discover lake after lake. (45)

There is nobody who is mine,
I am of no one, Kabir says;
Whoever this creation did create
In the same it assimilates. (46)

51. Of a Man Sans Guru

Let crores of moons and thousand crores
Of suns in the sky rise and shine,
For a man without true guru
Darkness doth reign around the clime. (1)

Hid by curtain the aphrodisian
Listens not what the guru talks;
So she's rather a female pig
Who loiters with body exposed. (2)

52. Of Selfishness

The selfish are kins in delight,
In grief they keep far and distant,
The philanthropists, says Kabir,
Pleasure or pain, are always present. (1)

53. Of Philanthropy

For the sake of my own I may
Rather die than ask for alms,
But for the well-being of others,
Of my shame I have no qualms. (1)

वृक्ष कबहू न फल भखै, नदी न संचै नीर।
परमारथ के कारने, साधुन धरयों शरीर॥ (2)

54. प्रेम कौ अंग

जा घट प्रेम न संचरै, सो घट जानु मसान।
जैसे खाल लुहार की, स्वाँस लेत बिनु प्रान॥ (1)

जहाँ प्रेम तहाँ नेम नहिं, तहाँ न बुधि व्यवहार।
प्रेम मगन मन भया, कौन गिने तिथि बार॥ (2)

पीया चाहे प्रेम रस, राखा चाहे मान।
दोइ खग इक म्यान में, देखया सुना न कान॥ (3)

55. पतिव्रता कौ अंग

पतिब्रता के एक है, व्यभिचारिन के दोय।
पतिब्रता व्यभिचारिणी, कहुँ क्यों मेला होय॥ (1)

पतिब्रता को सुख घना, जाके पति है एक।
मन मैली व्यभिचारिणी, ताकै खसम अनेक॥ (2)

एकें साधे सब सधे, सब साधै यक जाय।
जो तू सींचे मूल को, फूले फलै अघाय॥ (3)

Trees never eat fruits that they bear,
Their own waters rivers don't stock,
For the general good of 'thers,
Bodily form the righteous adopt. (2)

54. Of Love

Heart with no sensation of love!
Know that heart a cremation-site[1],
Like the hide of an ironsmith
Breathes in and out without life. (1)

Rules are ruled out where there is love,
Observance lacks rational way;
Heart engrossed in intense love
Is unmindful of date and day.[2] (2)

Dost thou wish for drinking love-juice
Together with keeping thy pride?
Single scabbard sheathing two swords—
Not heard with ears, nor seen with eyes. (3)

55. Of Loyal Wife

The loyal wife has one husband
Whereas two the adulteress has,
The loyal wife and adulteress!—
How can the two a concord have? (1)

The loyal wife with one husband
Hath intensity of pleasure;
The guilt-ridden adulteress
Hath many an adulterer. (2)

Handling one is to handle all,
In handling many one doth fleet;
If thou watereth the tree's root
It blooms and bears fruit to surfeit. (3)

मैं सेवक समरत्थ का, कबहुँ न होय अकाज।
पतिब्रता नाँगी रहे, वाही पति की लाज॥ (4)

56. आनदेव[1] कौ अंग

सौ बरसाँ भक्ति करै, एक दिन पूजै आनि।
सौ अपराधी आत्मा, परै चौरासी खानि॥ (1)

राम नाम को छाँड़िकै, करै अन्य की आस।
कहै कबीर ता दास का, होय नरक में बास॥ (2)

57. अमन[1] कौ अंग

पहले यह मन काग था, जीवन करता घात।
अब यह मन हंसा भया, मोती चुगि चुगि खात॥ (1)

58. मान कौ अंग

मान बड़ाई जगत में, कूकर की पहिचानि।
प्यार किया मुख चाटई, बैर किये ते हानि॥ (1)

बड़ा हुआ तो क्या हुआ, जैसी पेड़ खजूर।
पंथी छाँह न बैठही, फल लागै तो दूरि॥ (2)

I'm devotee of Omnipotent
So not to suffer loss or pain;
If the loyal wife is naked
It's not her but her husband's shame. (4)

56. Of Alien God

After his hundred years devotion
Who once alien god doth adore,
His soul's charged of a hundred crimes,
Thus he falls into mines eighty-four.[1] (1)

Setting aside the name of Ram
Who pins his hope on alien god[2],
Such a devotee, says Kabir,
Has the nether world for abode. (2)

57. Of Peace

Formerly my heart was a crow
Which used to kill the living (birds),
Now my heart has become a swan
That one by one pecks and eats pearls. (1)

58. Of Vainglory

Vainglorious praise in the world
Marks identity of a dog,
If pet, rises to lick the face,
If antagonised, harm doth cause. (1)

What boots it being highly tall
Much similar to the palm trees?
In its shade doesn't sit the pedestrian,
And fruits do stick too high to reach. (2)

59. संतोष कौ अंग

गोधन गजधन बाजिधन, और रतनधन खानि।
जब आवै संतोष धन, सब धन धूरि समानि॥ (1)

60. क्षमा कौ अंग

क्षमा बड़न को चाहिये, छोटन को उत्पात।
कहा विष्णु को घटि गयो, जो भृगु मारी लात॥ (1)

जहाँ दया तहँ धर्म[1] है, जहाँ लोभ तहँ पाप।
जहाँ क्रोध तहँ काल है, जहाँ क्षमा तहँ आप॥ (2)

61. देखादेखी[1] कौ अंग

देखादेखी भक्ति का कबहुँ न लागै रंग।
विपति परै यौ छाँड़ि सी, जिमि काँचली भुवंग॥ (1)

62. मध्य कौ अंग

हिंदू कहूँ तो मैं नहीं, मुसलमान भी नाँहि।
पाँच तत्व का पूतला, गैबी खेले माँहि॥ (1)

59. Of Contentment

Cow rich, elaphant-rich, horse-rich,
And rich treasures of precious stones,
All those riches are like the dust
Until to man contentment homes. (1)

60. Of Pardon

Pardon suits the magnanimous,
One who is low, mischiefs befit;
Speak! in what way did Vishnu lose
When Bhrigu[1] a kick did Him hit. (1)

Where there's mercy there's religion;
Where there's avarice there is sin;
Where there is anger there is Death,
Where there's pardon there God dwells in. (2)

61. Of Hearsay

The colour of that devotion
Does not adhere which's hearsay based,
In catastrophe it forsakes
The way slough is cast off by snake. (1)

62. Of the Middle

If I say I'm Hindu, I'm not,
Nor do as well a Muslim I'm,
I'm an effigy of five elements,
And in me plays the spark divine. (1)

अति का भला न बोलना, अति की भली न चूप।
अति का भला न बरसना, अति की भली न धूप॥ (2)

63. विचार कौ अंग

ज्यौं आवै त्योंही कहै, बोले नहीं बिचारि।
हतै पराई आतमा, जीभ लेइ तरवारि॥ (1)

64. दुविधा कौ अंग

राम नाम कडुवा लगै, मीठा लागै दाम।
दुविधा मैं दोऊ गया, माया मिली न राम॥ (1)

हृदये मैं है आरसी, मुख देखा नहिं जाय।
मुख तौ तबहीं देखई, दुविधा देह बहाय॥ (2)

65. ऐक्यता कौ अंग

राम रहीमा एक है, नाम धराया दोय।
कहै कबीर दो नाम सुनि, भर्मि परै मत कोय॥ (1)

कृष्णा करीमा एक है, नाम धराया दोय।
कहै कबीर दो नाम सुनि, भर्मि परै मत कोय॥ (2)

It's not good in excess to speak,
Nor is good in excess to keep mum,
To rain in excess is not good,
Nor is good the excess of sun. (2)

63. Of Thinking

Who utters as wells forth to tongue
Without thinking what he doth say,
Holding the sword of his tongue in hand
The souls of others he doth slay. (1)

64. Of Equivocal Mind

Whom the name of Ram tastes bitter
And plenty of money tastes pleasant,;
In equivocal state go both-
He gets neither maya nor Ram. (1)

In heart itself lies the mirror,
But one can't see one's face (mirrored on),
The (mirrored) face can be looked at
When equivoc'lity is gone. (2)

65. Of Oneness

Ram and Rahim are one and same,
Though named in two different ways,
Thus, hearing the two names pronounced,
Let none be deceived, Kabir says. (1)

Krishna and Kareema are one
Though named in two different ways,
Thus, hearing the two names pronounced,
Let none be deceived, Kabir says. (2)

66. पछतावा कौ अंग

अच्छा दिन पाछे गया, हरि सों किया न हेत।
अब पछतावै होत क्या, चिरिया खाया खेत॥ (1)

67. व्यापक कौ अंग

ज्यों तिल माँही तेल है, चकमक माँही आगि।
तेरा साँई तोहि में, जागि सकै तो जागि॥ (1)

68. मांसाहारी कौ अंग

बकरी पाती खात है, ताकी काढ़ी खाल।
जो बकरी को खात है, तिनका कौन हवाल॥ (1)

मुर्गी मुल्ला सौं कहै, जबह¹ करत है मोहिं।
साहब लेखा माँगसी, संकट परिहै तोहि॥ (2)

दिन को रोजा रहत है, रात हनत है गाय।
यह खून बह बंदगी, कहु क्यूँ खुशी खुदाय॥ (3)

कबिरा तेई पीर है, जो जानै पर पीर।
जो पर पीर न जानि है, सो काफिर बेपीर॥ (4)

66. Of Repentance

Good days of thine have gone backward,
Thou didst fail to grow love for God;
What's the use of repenting now!
When in field birds have eaten crop. (1)

67. Of the Universal

The way sesamus has oil within,
The way flintstone doth fire contain,
The same way thy God is within thee,
Wake up if thou canst be awake. (1)

68. Of the Non-Vegetarian

The goat eats grass and (leaves of trees)
But is killed and its skin peeled,
In what measure the men be dealt
Who kill the goat and its flesh eat? (1)

The hen to the Mullah sayeth:
'For thy food thou dost slaughter me;
When Saheb asks for thy account
Catastrophe will fall on thee'. (2)

In day-time thou observeth fast
And dost slaughter cow in the night;
This bloodshed! that adoration!
Say in what way it's God's delight? (3)

He alone is the Pir[1] who is
Full sensitive to others pain;
A cruel infidel he is who's
Insensitive to others pain. (4)

69. अनिंदा को अंग

दोरव पराया देखि करि, चलै हंसत हंसत।
अपना याद न आवई, जाकी आदि न अंत॥ (1)

तिनका कबहु न निंदिये, जों पाँव तले है सोय।
कबहू उड़ि आँखों परै, तो पीर घनेरी होय॥ (2)

आपण को न सराहिए, पर निंदिये न कोय।
अजहूँ लंबा धौहरा, ना जानो क्या होय॥ (3)

आपण पौ न सराहिए, और न कहिये रंक।
क्या जानो किहि ब्रिष तलि, कूड़ा होइ करंक॥ (4)

70. अनस्वादी कौ अंग

रूखा सूखा¹ खाइके, ठंडा पानी पीव।
देखि बिरानी चौंपड़ी², मत ललचावै जीव॥ (1)

आधी अरू रूखी भली, सारी सोग संताप।
जो चाहैगा चौंपड़ी, तौ बहुरि करेगा पाप॥ (2)

कबिरा साँई मुझको, रूखी रोटी देय।
चुपड़ी मांगत मैं डरूँ, मत रूखी छिन लेय॥ (3)

69. Of Non-Vituperation

Seeing blemishes in others
Those who laugh and sarcastic tend,
They ignore their own blemishes
Which have no beginning nor end. (1)

Don't condemn a straw (of grass)
Which lowly lies under thy feet,
It may fly and fall into th' eyes,
Then, pain is felt in the extreme. (2)

Don't heap praises on thyself
And vituperate not others;
No one knows what may happen to
Thy body now tall and robust. (3)

Don't extol thyself so as to
Nickname others paltry and vain
Nobody knows under which tree
A bone the garbage may contain. (4)

70. Of the Non-Gourmet

Eat thy meals raw and unsavoured,
(In contentment) drink cool water;
Seeing others eat seasoned dishes,
Abstain from making thy mouth water. (1)

Better is half unbuttered bread
Than the full which's sorrow and pain.
Thy desire for the seasoned meals
Will lead thee commit sins in train. (2)

Meek and humble Kabir entreats
God for giving him unsavoured bread,
Since in asking for savoured one
He fears the unsavoured be snatched. (3)

71. विविध

मन पाँचों के बसि परा, मन के बसि नहिं पाँच।
जित देखों तित दौं लगी, जित भागों तिति आँच॥ (1)

मन के हारे हार है, मन के जीते जीत।
कहै कबीर हरि पाइये, मन ही की परतीत॥ (2)

नारी कूड़ी नरक की, बिरला थामै बाग।
कोई साधू जन ऊबरा, सब जग मूवा लागि॥ (3)

एक कनक और कामिनी, ये लंबी तरवारि।
चालै थे हरि मिलन को, बिच ही लीन्हा मारि॥ (4)

नारी नदी अथाह जल, बूड़ि मुवा संसार।
ऐसा साधू ना मिले, जासौं उतरे पार॥ (5)

गाय भैंस घोड़ी गधी, नारी नाम है तास।
जा मंदिर मैं ये बसे, तहाँ न कीजै वास॥ (6)

जहाँ काम तहाँ राम नहिं, राम तहाँ नहिं काम।
दोऊ कबहू ना रहै, काम राम एक ठाम॥ (7)

कामी तो निर्भय भया, करै न काहू शंक।
इन्द्री केरे बस परा, भुगतै नरक निशंक॥ (8)

71. The Miscellaneous

Heart's subjugated by the five[1],
Heart does not the five subjugate,
Wherever I see there is fire,
Wherever I run there's fire-flame. (1)

There's defeat when the heart feels defeat,
There is victory when the heart wins,
God is realized, so says Kabir,
When heart to itself doth evince. (2)

Woman is a pool placed in hell,
Rare a man who his reins can hold,
A few righteous men may escape,
But diving dies the world wholesole. (3)

The gold and the aphrodisian,
Either of two is a long sword,
In the midway they kill the men
Who have set out for meeting God. (4)

Woman's river's water in spate,
In which the whole world sank and died,
No righteous man was ever found
Who could ferry to other side. (5)

Cow, buffalo, mare and she-ass,
Of female nomenclature are all,
In whatever house they dwell in
Thou must not dwell therein at all. (6)

Where there is lust there is no Ram,
Where there is Ram there is no lust,
At a single place, both of them—
Ram and lust—never co-exist. (7)

The lusty man lives without fear,
Of suspicions he bears no trace,
Since he is slave to sex desires,
No doubt, hell tortures he's to face. (8)

कूप पराया आपनाँ, गिरै बूड़ि जो जाय।
ऐसा भेद विचारिके, कुमति हि गोता खाय॥ (9)

काम क्रोध मद लोभ की, जब लग घट में खानि।
कहा मूर्ख कहा पंडिता, दोनों एक समानि॥ (10)

छोटी मोटी कामिनी, सब ही विष की बेल।
बैरी सारे दाव दै, वह मारे हँसि खेल॥ (11)

नागिन के तो दोय फन, नारी के फन बीस।
जाको डस्यो न फिरि जिये, मरि है बिस्वा बीस॥ (12)

कबीर सब जग यौं भ्रम्या फिरै ज्यूँ रामे को रोज।
सतगुरू थे सोधी भई, तब पाया हरि का षोज॥ (13)

कबीर खेति किसाण का, म्रगौं खाया झाड़ि।
खेत विचारा क्या करें, जो खसम न करई बाड़ि॥ (14)

कबीर नाव जरजरी, भरी विराँणै भारि।
खेवट सों परचा नहीं, क्यों करि उतरे पारि॥ (15)

कबीर पगड़ा दूरि है, जिनके बिच है राति।
का जाणैं का होइगा, उगवै तैं परभाति॥ (16)

माया काल की खाँणि है, धरि त्रिगुणी विपरीति।
जहाँ जाइ तहाँ सुख नहीं, यह माया की रीति॥ (17)

Grabbing other's well as one's own
One who doth fall and sink in it,
Having thought such a mystery
Only the vicious takes a dip. (9)

When a man becomes the quarry
Of lust, avarice and anger,
Whether a fool or a pundit,
Both are equal to each other. (10)

The aphrodisian, high or low,
All are a venomous creeper,
The foe uses all his tactics,
But she kills in playful laughter. (11)

A she-snake[2] has only two fangs,
While twenty fangs a woman has,
Those men she stings do not survive
And twenty times twenty go dead. (12)

Like a forest beast, I wander'd
All the world over, Kabir says;
Having discovered a true guru
Discovery of God I made. (13)

The peasant's field was grazed cleansweep
By a horde of deers, Kabir says,
What the pitiable field may do?
The husbandman had not it paled. (14)

This boat is worn out, says Kabir,
Burdened with things irrelevant,
Unacquainted with the Rower
How can it land the other end? (15)

For long is the path, says Kabir,
In the midst of which falls the night,
No one wotteth what will happen
Till morning before the sun's rise? (16)

A deep mine of death is maya
Which's three properties of contrast;
Maya has set this tradition—
Where she goes—happiness departs. (17)

हसती चढ़िया ज्ञान कै, सहज दुलीचा डारि।
स्वान रूप संसार है, पड्या भुसौ झषि मारि॥ (18)

कबीर मरों पे माँगौ नहीं, अपणै तन के काज।
परमारथ के कारणैं, मोहि माँगत न आवै लाज॥ (19)

चत्र भुजा के ध्यान में ब्रिजवासी सब संत।
कबीर मगन ता रूप मैं, जाके भुजा अनंत॥ (20)

बुरा बुरा सबको कहै, बुरा न दीखे कोइ।
जे दिल खोजों आपणी, मुझ सा बुरा न कोइ॥ (21)

रोड़ा भया तो क्या भया, पंथी को दुख देइ।
हरिजन ऐसा चाहिये, जिसी जिमीं की खेह॥ (22)

जुरा कूती जोबन ससा, काल अहेड़ी बार।
पलक बिना मैं पाकड़ै, गरब्यों कहा गंवार॥ (23)

मालन आवत देखि करि, कलियाँ करी पुकार।
फूले फूले चुणि लिये, काल्हि हमारी बार॥ (24)

बाढ़ी आवत देखि करि, तरवर डोलन लाग।
हम कटे की कुछ नहीं, पँखेरू घर भाग॥ (25)

फागुण आवत देखि करि, बन रूना मन माँहि।
ऊँची डाली पात है, दिन दिन पीले थाँहि॥ (26)

Ride the elephant of wisdom
The innate carpet having laid;
The whole world has semblance of dogs
Which go on barking all in vain. (18)

For my own body's sake I may
Rather die than beg, Kabir says,
But for the well-being of others
I shall not feel a trace of shame. (19)

Meditating He, the Four-Armed,[3]
The residents of Brij[4] are saints;
Kabir's delighted in the Form[5]
Whose arms are in unending train. (20)

The bad labels bad all and sundry,
But no one who is bad I see,
As much as I do introspect,
There is no one so bad like me. (21)

What is the use of stumbling-block?
Which to the pedestrian gives pain;
Such man-of-God we are in need
Who's like dust lying on pathways. (22)

Old age is bitch and youth is hare,
Tip-toed for assault is Time-poacher,
Who in a moment doth lay the seize;
Then why shouldst thou be vain, O boor? (23)

On seeing the gardener's wife come
Shout aloud the buds that are young,
'All flowers in bloom are picked up
So tomorrow will be our turn'. (24)

On seeing the tree-feller come
The tree in terror starts to shake:
'It doth not matter if I'm felled,
O bird, homeward thy flight take'. (25)

Seeing the month of Phagun[6] come,
In his heart of heart the tree weeps:
'My branches are tall but my leaves
Grow pale as day after day creeps'. (26)

पात पड़ंता यौं कहै, सुनि तरवर वनराइ।
अबके बिछुड़ै ना मिलें, कहिं दूरि पड़ेंगे जाइ॥ (27)

मेरा बीर लुहारिया, तू जिनि जालै मोहि।
इक दिन ऐसा होइगा, हूँ जालौंगी तोहि॥ (28)

मूरों कौं का रोइये, जो अपणौं घर जाइ।
रोइये बंदीवान को, जो हाटैं हाट बिकाइ॥ (29)

बाग बिछिटे म्रिग लौं, तिहि जिनें मारै कोइ।
आपै ही मर जाइसी, डाँवा डोला होइ॥ (30)

हरि दरियाँ सूभर भरियाँ, दरिया वार न पार।
खालिक बिना खाली नहीं, जेता सूई संचार॥ (31)

कबीर बेड़ा जरजरा फूटे छेक हजार।
हरूये हरूये तिरि गए, डूबे जिनि सिर भार॥ (32)

कबीर कोठी काठ की, दहुँ दिसि लागी आगि।
पंडित पंडित जल गुए, मूरख उबरे भागि॥ (33)

कौड़ी कौड़ी जोरि के, जोरें लाख करोरि।
चलती बार न कछु मिल्या, लई लंगोटी छोरि॥ (34)

कबीर संगति साध की, दिन दिन दूना हेतु।
साकत कारी काँवरी, धोए होइ न सेतु॥ (35)

The falling leaf exclaims thus:
'O thou Forest Lord! hark! this time's
My parting from thee is forever—
I'll fall far away in some slime'. (27)

'O brave ironsmith', says fuelwood,
'Don't set me ablaze, I tell thee;
A day is certain to come by
When thou wilt be set ablaze by me'. (28)

Why should we bewail for the dead?
Because to his own home he goes;
Bewail for the slave of desires
'In the worldly market who's sold. (29)

Let nobody kill the deer that
Has strayed away from the forest,
In roaming and wandering state
Of his own he will meet his death. (30)

The God-sea is full to the brim,
That sea has no beginning nor end,
No space is vacant without God
Even for a needle's movement. (31)

This boat is worn out, Kabir says,
Which has cracked in a thousand holes;
They could sail who were light in weight,
But sank who on their heads had load. (32)

Timber-made is this (body) house,
From ten directions[7] fire ablaze,
The learned pundits died in fire
But fools ran away in escape. (33)

Hoarding wealth cowries by cowries[8]
It did swell to thousand and millions,
Empty-handed when one departs,
All's left here even cloth for loins. (34)

The company of the righteous
Doubles day by day, says Kabir,
The *shaakt* is a rug, dark and black,
Which does not get white though washed neat (35)

Notes

1. Of Guru the Deity (p.21)

1. Kabir has frequently and repeatedly used the prefix 'sat' which is equal to 'eu' prefix of Greek language. In this transversion 'true' is used as Rabindranath Tagore has used it so. G.N. Das uses the word 'preceptor'.
2. Sixty-four lamps mean 64 arts.
3. Fourteen moons represent fourteen branches of knowledge.
4. Govind is a synonym of God. This word is usually used for Lord Krishna.
5. Maya, originally a word of Sanskrit language, has been adopted by English dictionary. *Oxford Universal Dictionary Illustrated* defines 'maya' as 'illusion', 'a prominent word of Hindu philosophy'. Maya, feminine in gender, is an abstraction but is mostly personified. The word, thus, means: love, affection, familial ties or attachment, mother, father, wife, son, daughter, pride, fame, worldly possessions and so on.

2. Of Remembering God (pp. 23-25)

1. In Hindu mythology, the Great Deluge came when Four-Headed Brahma, the Creator, was asleep.
2. Ten apertures are: two eyes, two ears, two nose-holes, mouth, anus, urinary hole and suture.
3. See note 1 under the heading "Of Maya"

5. Of Communion (with .God) (p. 29)

1. In its original version, this couplet of Kabir is very popular in the *antyaksree* (one of the sixty-four arts) defined as "reciting a verse beginning with the same letter which is the final letter of verse recited by another person". Further, this verse in its original version has a female

speaker, say a protagonist, as is indicated by the inflexion of verbs used. There is no unanimity in the meaning of the couplet. New criticism praises ambiguity of meaning as it has richness of meaning.

8. Of Portent (p. 33-37)

1. In Indian music there are seven notes, say basic alphabets of music.
2. Yamā is the god of death in Hindu mythology.
3. In the Hindu calendar, day and night, i.e. a single revolution of the sun on its axis is divided into eight parts of three hours each for which 'triad' is used.

9. Of Heart (Full of Desires) (p. 39)

1. Five bad companions are: lust, wrath, greed, attachment, and jealousy.

12. Of Maya (p. 41-45)

1. "The Triple" allude to *Sattwan, Rajas* and *Tamas* i.e. soothfastness, passion and ignorance.

13. Of the Shrewd (Brahmin) (pp. 45-47)

1. Word (with capital 'W') used in this book means (a) the knowledge and wisdom imparted by a guru, exhortations, (b) the heavenly Word of God's law, (c) teaching of an experienced saint, as the context may imply or suggest.
2. Saheb is a word of Arabic origin which means Master and is synonymous to God.
3. In Hindu rituals a brahmin acts as a priest and the person for whom the ritual is done is called 'yajman.'
4. Sacred thread worn by a Hindu is made of cotton yarn. The ring-shaped thread of usually 6 plies is the *sine quo non* of a Hindu. The sacred thread has a great religious significance. Of late, many Hindus are not worried about putting on the sacred thread.
5. Man's soul which does not get salvation has to undergo eighty-four lakh lives of beasts, brutes, birds, insects as punishment of sins.

6. In the Hindu myths, the whole creation is classified into four Great Ages (i) Satyug, (ii) Treta, (iii) Dwapar, and (iv) Kalyug. The last is associated with increase in crimes and decline in religious consciousness or righteousness.

15. Of Words Sans Deeds (p. 49)

1. In Devnagari script there are 52 alphabets—16 vowels and 36 consonants. Four alphabets are now obsolete.

16. Of Lusty Man and Of Lust (pp. 49-51)

1. The three worlds in Hindu myths are almost identical to what Dante meant by paradise, purgatory and hell.
2. In Hindi language feminine gender is expressed by inflexion so for the purpose of Kabir 'she-serpent' is used here.
3. The famous mythological story of Ram originally told by Balmiki and retold by Tulsidas in post-Kabir period centres around the epic war between Ram of Ayodhya and Ravana of Lanka (present-day Ceylon). The immediate cause of the war was the stealthy kidnapping of Ram's wife Sita. Ravana, the ten-headed, was killed in the war. Kabir is alluding to Sita's captivity by Ravana.

17. Of Truth (pp. 51-53)

1. This is used in the same sense as Milton in the line 'and present/My true account, lest He returning chide'. (Sonnet often entitled "On His Blindness".
2. Kabir refers to men of trading and business class with money and material possessions. They are usually non-vegetarians and epicureans.

20. Of Bad Company (p. 59)

1. A heavenly drop called 'swāti' falling in the mouths of banana, oyster and snake results in three different ways i.e. in banana it creates camphor, in oyster it begets pearl and in snake it breeds poison. This is a poetic belief based on myths.
2. A *shaakt* is a worshipper of Goddess Durga in all her forms and incarnations. Slaughter of animals for sacri-

fice is a common practice among *shaakts*. In the particular context it means a robust and healthy man.

25. Of Magnitude of the Righteous (p. 65-67)

1. The worshippers of Lord Vishnu are called the *vaishnavas*. This religious sect of Hindus is known for non-violent attitude marked with total abstinence from eggs, animal meat in any form and alcoholic drinks. They even abstain from onion and garlic.

2. Kabir's own name implies great, excellent or glorious.

28. Of Exhortations (p. 69)

1. Ironsmiths used hides of dead animals for blowing their fires ablaze. The practice is dying down because of electricity and other inventions.

29. Of Faith (p. 71)

1. Raghunath is used for Lord Ram. In its present sense it means bounteous God.

30. Of Identifying the Lover (God) (p. 71)

1. Kabir did not believe in incarnation so the verse has the description of Kabir's Abstract or Unconditioned God.

32. Of Potence (p. 73)

1. In Hindu myths seven seas are frequently mentioned. These are of (i) milk (ii) curd (iii) ghee (iv) salt (v) sugarcane juice (vi) liquor (vii) water.

39. Of Bravery (p. 79)

1. 'Aunt' here means 'mother's sister'. The original word 'khālā' implies a prostitute as well. In English too, 'aunt' has similar connotation.

40. Of Time/ Death (pp. 81-85)

1. Kabir has used 'Kāl' which means Time (with capital 'T') often used in Shakespeare's sonnets, e.g. 'Love's not Time's fool, though rosy lips and cheeks' (Sonnet no. 116, line 9).

2. In Kabir's times clocks were not common as they are today. Kabir has, therefore, referred to the clock at the king's court.

3. In the *Manusmriti* the dead body is quarantined and treated as untouchable. The mourners show haste in taking the dead body for cremation (by burning on the pyre).

44. Of Origin of Devotion (p. 91)

1. In Hindu myths Meru or Sumeru is the highest mountain in the world.

45. Of the Musk Deer (p. 91)

1. Singhal Island refers to Ceylon of today. Lord Ram conquered Ravana so a place of pilgrimage.

50. Of the Indivisible (pp. 97-107)

1. Alludes to Prithu the mighty king in Hindu mythology. Prithu is known for levelling the uneven earth.

2. Alludes to the heroic sons of Sagar. Sagar, the ancestor of Lord Ram, was a mighty king who celebrated his victories by holding *Ashwamedh Yagna*. When Sagar let loose the horse, it was hidden underground near the sea. The sons of Sagar split apart the sea to find out the horse. The tale further tells the death of Sagar's sixty-thousand sons cursed by Gautam Rishi. Bhagirath, the great grandson of Sagar, brought the sacred river Ganges on the earth for the salvation of his sixty thousand ancestors.

3. Alludes to Ravana, the famous king of Lanka, who in Hindu myths, is said to have lifted the mountain Kailash in his arms to weigh it.

4. It refers to *Sati Pratha* prevalent in India. On the death of the husband his wife either voluntarily burnt herself on the pyre of her husband or was forcibly burnt by her in-laws and relatives.

5. Sheikh Taki was a famous Muslim Pir or saint who was contemporary to Kabir. In the brief biography of Kabir mention to Sheikh Taki is made.

54. Of Love (p. 109)

1. A cremation-site is the place where Hindus burn dead bodies. In the Hindu psyche a cremation-site is usually associated with sepulchral silence and haunting of ghosts.
2. Visits of friends and relatives are good and auspicious on certain days of a week. Tuesday and Saturday are usually avoided for visits of well-wishing friends and relatives.

56. Of Alien God (p.111)

1. Eighty-four alludes to eighty-four lakh lives of birds, beasts, birds and animals that a sinner has to live as the punishment of his sins. Worshipping an alien god in the opinion of Kabir is a sin.
2. Alien god here means any other god except the Unconditioned God of Kabir's concept. Hindus are polytheists, sometimes called 'pagans'. It seems proper to quote from the Bible: "They foresook the Lord and served the Ba'als; they went after other gods, from among the gods of peoples and were round about them, and bowed down to them....But yet they didn't listen to their judges; for they played the harlot after other gods and bowed down to them." *Judges*, 2).

60. Of Pardon (p.113)

1. In the *Padma Puran* the mythical tale of Bhrigu stamping a kick on the breast of Lord Vishnu is narrated. Manu and other sages of great ascetic powers were to decide "Who is the best of the divinities worthy of being worshipped by brahmans, who knew the Veds." They sent Bhrigu on this mission. Bhrigu went to Shiva and then to Brahma but to both of them he cursed. He then went to Vishnu and with his left foot stamped a kick on Vishnu's breast. Lord Vishnu, instead of being provoked to vengeance, regarded the touch of Bhrigu's foot as blessing and particles of dust falling from Bhrigu's foot as purification. Bhrigu was full of joy so shed his tears. On return to the sages he reported that Lord Vishnu was

the best of all divinities and worthy to be worshipped by brahmans.

68. Of the Non-Vegetarian (p. 117)

1. Pir means a Muslim saint. The word has been adopted by English dictionary. Kabir plays pun on the word 'pir' which in Hindi means 'pain'.

72. The Miscellaneous (pp. 121-127)

1. Lust, wrath, pride, greed and attachment are five bad companions.
2. In Hindi language feminine gender is expressed by inflexion. Kabir intends it to be feminine.
3. The Four-Armed is Lord Vishnu but here it means Lord Krishna who was the incarnation of Lord Vishnu.
4. Brij is the place of Lord Krishna's childhood and boyhood. This place is in district Mathura of Uttar Pradesh state.
5. Refers to the Unconditioned God of Kabir.
6. *Phagun* is the last month of Hindu calendar which is from mid-February to mid-March. In the early spring so many trees shed their old leaves to give way to new ones.
7. In Hindu scriptures ten directions are often referred to. These are: east, west, north, south, north-east, north-west, south-east, south-west, up and down.
8. Sea-shells were used as coins of perhaps lowest denomination.

GLOSSARY (Of Hindi Words)

1. गुरुदेव कौ अंग

1. गुरु is now an English word. Guru is a religious teacher belonging to the Ahram system of education in India. Kabir deifies the guru so a true guru is like a deity or god. Kabir has time and again used the prefix 'sət' which

means 'good'. Tagore has used 'true' for this prefix so throughout this transversion 'true' is used where the prefix 'sət' is used.

2. अंग literally means 'body' or 'bodily limb'. The couplets of the *Sakhi* are classified into corpuses as the titles suggest. This word in the classification means 'characteristics' or 'defining characteristics' of the heading. The classification does not seem absolutely correct as in the heading "Of the Indivisible" the couplets belong to several characteristics. In this transversion 'Of' is used as is used by Bacon and Cowley for the titles of essays.

3. ⸱ सद्गुरु See note 1.

4. सोधी means learned, wise and generous in the context.

5. हरि an epithet of God

6. हरिजन means the devotees or who believe in God.

7. लोक वेद means blindly following the Scriptures especially the Four Vedas (i) Rik (ii) Yaju (iii) Sam (iv) Atharwa. The word implies belief in rituals.

8. जती 'Jati' or 'Yati' means a fakir, an ascetic, an anchorite who has subdued his passions. 'Mendicant friar' may be an equivalent term.

2. सुमिरन कौ अंग

1. सुमिरन is a form of adoration of God. It means to recollect, to remember, to count beads and repeat the name of god.

2. गोविंद is an epithet of God, usually implies Lord Krishna.

3. माला means wreath, rosary, rosebeads.

4. भवसागर is used for the world as vast sea or ocean usually dark. It suggests the purgatory of Dante.

5. ओट literally means 'leeward' or 'leeway'. It means shelter or protection.

6. जोग 'Yog' is adopted by English dictionary. It means ascetism specially of the *Nathpanthis*.

3. विरह कौ अंग

1. विरहनि means separated from lover or husband. 'Grass-

widow' is the English word for it. For the purpose of versification 'love-lorn' is used. In Indian literatures, the wife or beloved separated from her lover or husband is a common subject-matter of poetry.

2. शब्द message from the lover. For its meanings see the note under the heading "Of the Word".

3. खाँड is raw sugar. Unrefined sugar, treacle, molasses, sweet or honey are the implied meanings according to context.

4. ग्यान विरह कौ अंग

1. ग्यान विरह the title may not seem exact. It means inward struggle because of wisdom descending on a man.

2. दौं literally means 'fire'. The fire figuratively is the fire of wisdom that descends on a devotee or a saint because of his devotion and taking the world as unreal or illusion.

3. आहेड़ी means 'poacher' or 'hunter'. Here it means the 'guru'.

4. मृग literally means 'deer' but it is the symbol of a disciple who is being weaned from his pleasures.

5. नदियाँ means rivers but here it means 'desires'.

6. मंछी literally means 'fish' but is the symbol of pure heart that has freed itself from desires. Fish ascending the tree suggests Kabir's philosophy of 'Endocrines'. Intellectual and spiritual pleasures have priority over sensual desires.

5. परचा कौ अंग

1. परचा may mean, in its simple sense, 'acquaintance' but it implies 'communion with God'.

2. पंषी literally means 'bird' but is the symbol of 'soul'.

3. प्यंड/पिंड means 'body' or 'physical body' with no soul.

4. परदेस symbolises this world because the soul goes to its permanent home in heavens.

5. अविनाशी is used as an epithet of God Who is immortal beyond the cycle of births and deaths.

6. सुख दुख In the translation of these two words 'delight and dole' is mostly used. 'Pleasure and pain' may be the other pair. 'Happiness and sorrow' may be the third preference. In the transversion, syllables in the particular line and the necessity of rhyming word is the guiding factor.

7. देस 'Land' is used after Tagore.

8. अलेख 'Invisible' is used here. It refers to Kabir's Unconditioned God.

9. लाली refers to the red-coloured radiance of Kabir's Unconditioned God.

6. जणाँ कौ अंग

1. जणाँ literally means 'old' or 'ancient', but suggests 'perpetual', 'permanent', and 'immortal'. 'Classic ancient' is the translator's coinage.

7. निहकर्मीं पतिव्रता कौ अंग

1. दोजग/ दोजख is a word of Persian language meaning 'hell'.

2. भिस्त is a word of Persian language meaning 'paradise'.

3. पतिव्रता means 'loyal wife' which implies chastity, purity and devotion.

8. चितावणी कौ अंग

1. चितावणी means the action of warning. English word 'portend' means 'to give warning of' and 'portent' means 'that which portends or foretells something about to happen, especially of a calamitous nature.'

2. नौबति beating of kettle-drums and playing on trumpet was a common feature in the king's palace and in the houses of rich men to denote good omen or festivity.

3. पट्टण means a 'town' specially a town inside a fort.

4. मंदिर literally means 'temples' but may mean 'house' or 'houses'

5. टेसू The blossom of *butae frandosa*. In early summer it blossoms in shining red colour.

6. काल This word is used for 'time', 'period', 'age' and 'death'. Capital 'T' is used when it means 'death' or suggests 'god of death'.

7. सैंबल is 'red silk cotton plant'.

8. सैंट means bricks and material for cementing bricks.

9. सैंवार means grass or weeds or both.

10. चेजारा means artisan. God is an artisan building this human body.

11. लाष means a 'lakh' or 'lac' meaning thereby very costly.

12. षेह means 'dust'.

13. धिगि means 'disdain', 'contempt', 'opprobrium'. It has an interjectory use in most cases.

14. धौलहर means a 'palace'.

15. मानि/ मान means 'vainglory' or 'pride'.

16. बलाइ a word of Arabic meaning 'fiend' which also means 'evil', 'calamity', 'pain' or 'disease'.

9. मन कौ अंग

1. मन This word is used by Kabir for 'heart which has worldly desires'.

2. जीव literally means any living being but means 'man' or 'human being'.

3. कुसलात In several couplets of Kabir this word is used. This word suggests a dramatic situation. When two relatives, friends or close acquaintances meet after a gap of time, after proper salutation, well-being of each other is asked by each other.

4. जम means 'Yama' the God of Death.

5. पंच कुसंगी Five bad companions are: lust, wrath, greed, pride and attachment.

6. मैंगल means an elephant 'run amuck'.

10. सूषिम मारग कौ अंग

1. सूषिम literally means 'subtle' but suggests metaphysical existence above and beyond this physical existence.

11. सूषिम जनम कौ अंग

1. जनम The word has metaphysical dimensions. After physical death there is spiritual rebirth, or, man has spiritual life beyond the trivial human existence.

12. माया कौ अंग

1. माया See note 5 under the heading "Of Guru the Deity."

2. कामिणीं means a 'lusty woman'. The word 'aphrodisian' is used because the word suggests sexually exciting like the physical beauty of Aphrodite.

3. बुगली is a female 'crane'. The word is the symbol of maya that pollutes spiritual life.

4. सायर means 'sea' symbolising human body.

5. हंस is the symbol of a devotee who has controlled his desires and passions.

13. चाणक कौ अंग

1. चाणक means 'shrewd' or 'cunning'. The word is said to be derived from the name of Chanakya in the fourth century B.C. He was a shrewd Brahmin and was instrumental in making Chandra Gupta the king and later emperor.

2. पंडित is an English word now. In the times of Kabir brahmin pundits were read in scriptures and they were instrumental in perpetuating rituals which Kabir satirized.

3. मसालची A torch-bearer (not the present-day electric or battery torch) was a man carrying lighted pots or burning sticks.

4. यजमान means a 'client' in the ritual performed by a brahmin as priest.

5. आनदेव means 'alien god'. See note 2 under the heading "Of Alien God".

6. जनेऊ See note 4 under the heading "Of the Shrewd (Brahmin)"

7. चौरासी See note 1 under the heading "Of Alien God".

14. करणीं बिना कथनी कौ अंग

1. कालबूत is a framework for constructing a kupola, grand-looking but subject to coming down in ruins.

17. साँच कौ अंग

1. साह is a Persian word meaning 'Shah' or 'king'.
2. लेखा See note 1 under the heading "Of Truth".

18. भ्रम विधौंसण कौ अंग

1. विधौंसण means 'destruction'. The word 'end' seemed sufficient.

19. भेष कौ अंग

1. सिद्धि means 'success' or 'completeness'. This word cannot have an English equivalent so 'accomplishments' is used.
2. अमरापुर means 'paradise'.

20. कुसंगति कौ अंग

1. साषित See note 2 under the heading "Of Bad Company".
2. नबेरि means a newly-wed bride so tender and delicate.

21. संगति कौ अंग

1. साधु means 'the righteous' or 'righteous man'. Tagore has used the original word 'Sadhu'. Kabir's poetry abounds in the use of this word. In the times of Kabir men belonging to some religious sect or school might be moving from place to place begging for alms for subsistence. People might have held them in high esteem. It seems pertinent to quote from the Bible: "He leads me in paths of righteousness"; he loves righteousness and justice"; "thy righteousness is like mountains of God"; "the wicked borrows but cannot pay back but righteousness is generous and gives"; "the righteous shall

possess the land" and "the mouth of the righteous utters wisdom and his tongue speaks justice". Kabir's couplets, more or less, speak the same things.

2. असाधु is the opposite of 'the righteous' so means 'wicked'.

22. असाध कौ अंग

1. असाध is the opposite of 'the righteous' so it means 'wicked'.

2. अतीत means who has controlled his passions and given up worldly desires. The word is generally used for a Jain saint.

23. साध कौ अंग

1. साधु See note 1 under the head "संगति कौ अंग"

24. साध साक्षीभूत कौ अंग

1. साक्षीभूत Metaphysical self when a man is in the fourth state called तुरीय. In ordinary human experience all human activities of psychological self take place in conscious, sub-conscious and un-conscious mind. The fourth is transcendent state in which a man is free from pride, wrath, greed, desires, passions and reaches a state of communion with God. That transcending state is the witness of all human activities from an exalted state and is unconcerned with all such things.

25. साध महिमां कौ अंग

1. महिमां The word 'magnitude' seems most proper though 'dignity', 'venerableness', 'greatness', 'majesty', 'exaltation' seem proper in one way or the other.

2. वैसनो See note 1 under the heading "Of the Magnitude of the Righteous"

3. साषत See note 2 under the heading "Of Bad Company".

4. मुड़हट See note 1 under the heading "Of Love".

5. पनिहारी means 'a woman who fetches water' or the 'wife of a man who fetches water' so poor and meek.

6. अऊत means 'without a son' or 'without son or daughter'.

31. विरकताई कौ अंग

1. मंदिल कंधि चढ़ाय is an idiomatic use meaning 'finding out a permanent home'.

32. संम्रथाई कौ अंग

1. साँई is usually used by Muslims for the lord, the master. Here it means 'God'.

34. सबद कौ अंग

1. सबद See note 1 under the heading "Of the Shrewd (Brahmin)".
2. सुरति In the context it means the Scriptures.

35. जीवन-मृतक कौ अंग

1. जीवन-मृतक means that man of saintly nature who has given up all desires and passions.
2. मर्जिवा This word is used for a diver who dives into the sea for precious stones so he hazards his life. In figurative use the word means a man who with his conscious mind has elevated himself from worldly desires and passions, so, though alive, he lives in death.

37. गुरुसिष हेरा कौ अंग

1. गुरुसिष हेरा The guru is in search of a true, worthy and receptive disciple and a would-be disciple is in search of a true guru.
2. सैन means a 'hint' or a 'clue'. In the context 'symbols' is used.
3. सुरति This word is used in so many meanings and senses by Kabir. Here it means perception with ears.

39. सूरातन कौ अंग

1. आनंद Sir Edwin Arnold uses 'joy' for this word.
2. खाला means 'mother's sister'. See note 1 under the heading "Of Bravery".

3. सीस उतारै हाथ करि is an idiomatic expression meaning 'bowing down the head', and, figuratively, 'by giving up vanity and pride'.

4. धड़ सूली सिर कंगुरै alludes to the system of executing to death placing on the gibbet and on beheading the head falling on the turret or wall.

40. काल कौ अंग

1. काल See note 1 under the heading "Of Time/Death".

2. खलक means 'the world' or 'worldly creature'.

3. चबीणा means 'food' or 'meal'.

4. तोरण आया बींद This expression suggests an arched gate. When the bride-groom reaches under the gate receiving hosts (mostly women) rush to him.

5. जगाति means 'Tax collector'. In the days of Kabir at the bank of a river the tax collectors might be collecting tax seeing headloads.

41. संजीवनी कौ अंग

1. संजीवनी is a drug that brings back a dead man to life. 'Elixir' prolongs life. In alchemy it is 'elixir vitae'.

44. उपजणि कौ अंग

1. उपजणि means 'origin of devotion to God'.

2. मेर means 'the feeling of one's own' and 'egotistic pride'. In the context 'familial ties' seems appropriate.

49. बेलि कौ अंग

1. बेलि means 'a creeping plant'. The word stands for worldly desires.

50. अबिहड़ कौ अंग

1. अबिहड़ means that cannot be divided so remains one.

2. अर्ब खर्ब The former word is equal to one hundred crores and the latter word means ten thousand crores. For the

purpose of versification 'millions and billions' is used which means 'countless'.

3. राउर means 'king's household'.

4. पोरवरि 'Lake' is used here which may also mean 'pond'. Symbolically, Kabir is alluding to so many minor gods. Kabir is against polytheism.

56. आनदेव कौ अंग

1. आनदेव means any other god except the Unconditioned God of Kabir. See note 1 under the head "Of Alien God".

57. अमन कौ अंग

1. अमन is 'peace' or 'tranquillity'. The word connotes a sense of prosperity as well.

60. क्षमा कौ अंग

1. धर्म 'Religion' is used which is a very common word.

61. देखादेखी कौ अंग

1. देखादेखी means 'imitative'. The context implies what is not based on experience or knowledge. 'Hearsay' seems proper.

68. मांसाहारी कौ अंग

1. जबह means 'slaughter' or 'killing an animal for food'. The use of words which are now called Urdu words gives a shade of meaning which cannot be reproduced in the same spirit.

71. अनस्वादी कौ अंग

1. रुखा-सूखा This word suggests the poverty of people. The use of butter and ghee was/is the symbol of well-to-do classes.

2. चौंपड़ी means 'ghee applied' in its literal sense.

Selected Bibliography

Arnold, Sir Edwin, *Bhagavad Gita: The Song Celestial,* Jaico (Bombay, 1994)

Baldick, Chris ed., *The Concise Oxford Dictionary of Literary Terms* OUP (Oxford, 1990)

Das, G.N. *Couplets From Kabir.* Motilal Banarsidass, (Delhi, 1999)

Drew, Elizabeth, "Imagery" in *Discovering Poetry* W.W.Norton Co. (New York, 1972)

Hess, Linda & Singh, Sukdev, *The Bijak of Kabir,* Motilal Banarsidass (Delhi, 1983).

Howe, Irving ed., *Modern Literary Criticism,* Beacon Press (Boston, 1958)

Johnson, Wendell Stacy, *The Critical Reader: Judging and Analysing Literature,* Frederick Unger Publishing Co. (New York, 1978)

Khayyam, Omar, *Rubaiyat of Omar Khayyam* in *Longer Poems Old and New* ed. A.S.Cairncross, Macmillan (New York, 1962)

Kittay, Eva Feder, *Metaphor: Its Cognitive Force and Linguistic Structure,* (Oxford, 1987)

Langbaum, Robert, *Poetry of Experience: The Dramatic Monologue in Modern Literary Tradition,* Penguin (Ontario, 1974)

Little, William, *The Oxford Universal Dictionary Illustrated,* Oxford, Clarendon Press (Oxford, 1976)

Misra, Dr. Bhagwat Swaroop, *Kabir Granthawali* (Hindi) Vinod Pustak Mandir (Agra 1987)

O'Connor, William Van, *Sense and Sensibility in Modern Poetry,* Gardiner Press (New York, 1973)

O'Flaherty, Wendy Doniger, *Hindu Myths,* Penguin Books of India (New Delhi, 1975)

Pandeya, Jagdish Chandra, *Darshan Kya Hai?* (Hindi) Pragati Prakashan (Delhi, 1988)

Richards, I.A., *Principles of Literary Criticism,* Routledge (London, 1963)

Singh, Jaidev, and, Singh, Vasudev, *Kabir Vani Peeyush* (Hindi), Vishwavidyalaya Prakashan (Varanasi, 1998)

Singh, Rajdev, *Santon Ka Bhaktiyog* (Hindi), Hindi Pracharak Sansthan (Varanasi 1988)

Singh, Vasudev, *Kabir Kavya Kosh* (Hindi) Vishwavidyalaya Prakashan (Varanasi, 1987)

Tagore, Rabindranath, "Poems of Kabir" in *English Writings of Tagore* (Photostat copy from Sahitya Academy Library, New Delhi)

Vaudeville, Charlotte, *Kavir,* Oxford University Press (Delhi, 1974).

Wimsatt, William K, and Brooks, Cleanth, *Literary Criticism: A Short History,* Oxford & IBH Publishing Co. (New Delhi, 1957)

Yugeshwar, Prof., *Kabir Samagra: Pratham Bhag* (Hindi) Pracharak Granthawali Pariyojana (Varanasi, 1995).

Note: This book containing all the *Dohas* of the *Sakhi* with introduction, notes, comments and glossary, has been the main source book for the transversion. The classification also is according to this book by Prof. Yugeshwar. Transversion of selections from couplets included in *Parishishts* (Appendices) A and B of *Kabir Samagra* have been included under the heading "The Miscellaneous" of the transversion.

Index of First Half-Lines in Hindi and Corresponding Index of First Lines in English